2/89

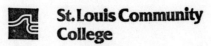

Fictions of
the Feminine

Fictions of the Feminine

PURITAN DOCTRINE AND THE REPRESENTATION OF WOMEN

Margaret Olofson Thickstun

Cornell University Press

ITHACA AND LONDON

CORNELL UNIVERSITY PRESS GRATEFULLY ACKNOWLEDGES
A GRANT FROM THE ANDREW W. MELLON FOUNDATION
THAT AIDED IN BRINGING THIS BOOK TO PUBLICATION.

Chapter 3 is a slightly revised version of my article of the
same title, which appeared in *Studies in English Literature, 1500–1900*,
26 (1986), copyright © William Marsh Rice University 1986.

First published 1988 by Cornell University Press.

International Standard Book Number 0-8014-2107-1
Library of Congress Catalog Card Number 87-25072

Printed in the United States of America
Librarians: Library of Congress cataloging information
appears on the last page of the book.

The paper in this book is acid-free and meets the guidelines for
permanence and durability of the Committee on Production Guidelines
for Book Longevity of the Council on Library Resources.

For Bill

Contents

Preface

The Protestant tradition that this book engages has transformed the intellectual and moral life of Western culture. In particular, a Protestant emphasis on conscience and individual responsibility has shaped the political thought and activity of Americans from John Winthrop to Henry David Thoreau and Martin Luther King. Because of its profound influence, this tradition informs the way we conduct our personal lives as well. It offers inspiring examples of moral heroism and seductive images of divinely sanctioned sexual hierarchy. The Puritan ideal of companionate marriage, with the husband as head of the household and the wife his loving helpmate, still conditions our understanding of marital relations. Because it presents hierarchy as an expression of loving compliance "requir'd with gentle sway / And by her yielded, by him best receiv'd" (*Paradise Lost* 4.308–9) and appeals to Scripture for its authority, this manifestation of sexism proves a slippery and stubborn adversary. But the Protestant tradition, in arguing for the dignity of the individual, the primacy of individual conscience, and the imperative of impassioned protest against injustice, also authorizes, even requires, a feminist critique of itself.

This book explores, from the perspective of such a critique, the influence of Puritan theology and domestic theory on the representation of women in English narrative. Spenser's *Faerie Queene*, Milton's *Paradise Lost*, and Bunyan's *Pilgrim's Progress* establish a recurrent pattern in which male protagonists displace female characters from their traditional roles as Brides of Christ and representatives of chastity. I argue that this pattern derives from Saint Paul's metaphorical understanding of gender relations—that male is to female as spirit is to flesh. In their domestic theory and in their literature, Puritan men use Paul's analogy to deflect their ambivalence about human frailty onto women. My introduction explores the contradictions within Paul's expression of the Gospel and considers how those contradictions shape Puritan ideas about women's roles and the possibility of female heroism. Subsequent chapters trace the development of those ideas in the major literature of the Puritan tradition and in two novels—Richardson's *Clarissa* and Hawthorne's *Scarlet Letter*—that respond critically to the conflation of female sexuality and spiritual inadequacy inherent in the Puritan texts.

Like all serious readers of Milton and his contemporaries, I aspire to become part of Milton's ideal, fit audience. But I do not believe that John Milton, an ardent spokesman for freedom of conscience and the responsibility of all individuals to engage in a sincere and earnest search after truth, would respect a docile reader. He demands for his readers "the liberty to know, to utter, and to argue freely according to conscience, above all other liberties" (*Areopagitica*). In *Womens Speaking Justified* (1667), Margaret Askew Fell Fox, one of the early advocates of the Quaker movement, challenges the idea of biblically authorized patriarchy by citing passages in which early Christian women prophesy and minister; like other dissenting women, she argues that the dispensation of grace cancels out the restrictions of law. Feminist biblical theologians continue to be engaged in reconstructing the role of women in the early Church as part of a hermeneutics aimed at the recovery of the genuine egalitarian nature of the Gospel and the movement toward a true democracy of believers. I am convinced, with these theologians, that the Christian tradition is not essentially sexist but only historically so. Like them, I see no need to abandon the texts that are our intellectual and spiritual heritage. We should instead, as Paul himself urges, "prove all things; hold fast that which is good" (1 Thess. 5.21).

I am grateful to the community of scholars and teachers who have encouraged and assisted me in my efforts to fulfill Paul's injunction. Mary Ann Radzinowicz, who directed this project at its earliest stage, has been unfailingly enthusiastic in her support and invaluably quick and thorough in her response to my written work. Michael Colacurcio shared not only his extensive knowledge of things Puritan but also his playful seriousness about things intellectual. I thank Jonathan Bishop for sharing both his understanding of the Pauline letters and his zeal for the truth. My readers at Cornell University Press, Diane McColley and Victoria Kahn, provided serious, detailed responses that, while a bit daunting, have helped me immeasurably to sharpen and strengthen my argument. Carol Kaske, Harry Shaw, and Jan Gallagher kindly read and commented on the chapters that fell within their expertise. I deeply regret that David Novarr, who provided so much help and encouragement during my graduate study, did not live to see this book in its final form.

I must also express my appreciation to a wider circle of scholars and teachers whose friendship and encouragement have influenced my intellectual and personal growth: Sarah Youngblood, Lynne Warrin, Evan Radcliffe, Nancy Shaw, Richard DuRocher, Karen Cherewatuk, and Lorraine Clark. My mother, Carolyn Olofson, has shown me the joy of a life dedicated to art and teaching, and my father, John Olofson, has taught me how beautiful and persuasive language can be. My husband, William Thickstun, has helped me more than anyone else with his patient criticism and support.

MARGARET OLOFSON THICKSTUN

New York, New York

Fictions of
the Feminine

Introduction: The Pauline Precedent for the Puritan View of Women

I

The literary presentation of women in English narratives changed dramatically during the seventeenth century. In Spenser's *Faerie Queene*, Milton's *Paradise Lost*, and Bunyan's *Pilgrim's Progress*, Part 2, a recurrent pattern emerges in which male protagonists displace females from the positive roles women traditionally inhabited and come to personify virtues women conventionally represented. In the first book of *The Faerie Queene*, Spenser distinguishes clearly between Una and Duessa, between the pure, good woman and the sexual, evil woman. Una wanders through Faery Land, alone and uncriticized, her virtue her sole and sufficient protection; similarly, the Lady in *Comus*, the one exceptional Puritan heroine, survives her ordeal in the forest with unblemished integrity, her mind and body inviolable. But when Bunyan's Christiana sets forth on her pilgrimage, a woman's virtue is no longer considered either adequate protection or adequate excuse for such independence. When she is sexually assaulted, both Christiana and her Reliever recognize her failure to secure a male guide as an indication that she secretly desired the assault. Her independence offends against a conception of women as necessarily subordinate because of their spiritual weakness and inferiority. The displacement of women and the subsumption of female virtues into a male ideal derive from the growing influence of Puritan thought on English culture; the ideal of sexual purity, traditionally a woman's greatest virtue, cannot coexist comfortably with an insistence on Original Sin. I want to consider the shift in Puritan literature from the polarized world of Madonna/Whore, Minerva/Medusa to a world in which each woman contains within herself both possibilities. I also want to explore, in *Clarissa* and *The Scarlet Letter,* two possible responses from within the tradition to the Puritan devaluation of womanhood.

For my purposes, I will use *Puritan* fairly broadly, to cover those elements of English Protestantism which stressed a true sight of sin, justification by faith alone, and the reformation of church and family government in the light of scriptural, especially Pauline, models.[1] In providing contexts and support for my discussion of the central texts, I ascribe equal authority to both Separating and Non-Separating, both English and Colonial American writers. Puritans of the late sixteenth century differed from other English Protestants more in degree of reformist fervency than in kind; Calvinist expressions of the doctrines of Original Sin, the limitations of Free Will in the unregenerate, and Justification by Faith form articles 9–11 of the Thirty-nine Articles of the Anglican church. Nor was there a doctrinal distinction between English and Massachusetts Bay Puritans in the early seventeenth century. The Massachusetts Bay colonists were Non-Separating Puritans, educated at English schools and ministers to English congregations before and after their emigration. They left England for America because they hoped to establish in the wilderness a model Christian community, "a city on a hill," which would lead to the reformation of

1. For intelligent, readable introductions to Puritanism, see Horton Davies, *Worship and Theology in England,* vol. 2, *From Andrews to Baxter* (Princeton: Princeton University Press, 1975), esp. pp. 112–129, and Edmund Morgan, *Visible Saints: The History of a Puritan Idea* (Ithaca: Cornell University Press, 1965). John S. Coolidge, in *The Pauline Renaissance in England: Puritanism and the Bible* (Oxford: Clarendon Press, 1970), discusses the debate over Christian liberty and edification between Anglican and Separatist theologians.

English society. With the advent of the Puritan Revolution, many colonists returned to England, just as many Puritans later fled England for New England at the collapse of the Puritan Commonwealth.

The hallmark of Puritan spirituality is anxiety and self-abasement. Horton Davies identifies Lewis Bayly's *Practise of Piety* (London, 1612) as "a model for Puritan and 'low church' devotion, by his recommendation that Bible study was as necessary as prayer and meditation." *The Practise of Piety*, an eight-hundred-page theological handbook that went through fifty-nine editions between 1612 and 1735, includes over forty pages of advice toward preparing to receive the Lord's Supper, beginning with a meditation "How to consider thine owne unworthinesse." The final prayer, "a sweet soliloquie to be said betwixt the consecration and receiving of the Sacrament," includes this expression of self-denigration as a means to encourage those anxious about their acceptance: "I am in a word, a *carnall* Creature, whose very soule is *'sold under sinne'*: a wretched man, compassed about with *a body of death*. Yet lord, seeing thou *callest*, here I come, and seeing thou callest *sinners*, I have thrust myself in among the rest, and seeing thou callest *all* with their *heaviest loades*, I see no reason why I should stay behinde."[2] Because belief in one's own worthiness proved an individual's sinful self-confidence, anxiety and doubt over one's spiritual status provided perhaps the only glimpse of assurance.

Placing the burden of salvation on the individual believer, Puritan practice required continuous self-examination and seeking after grace, yet denied one's ability to influence salvation in any way. With the new emphasis on a firsthand, intimate understanding of the Bible, the uncomfortable paradoxes of the doctrines of Original Sin and Justification by Faith became matters of popular and daily concern. Such sustained, intense uncertainty at times proved psychologically insupportable. John Winthrop, governor of Massachusetts Bay Colony, records an incident in which "a woman of Boston congregation,

2. Davies, *Worship and Theology*, 2:113–14; Lewis Bayly, *The Practise of Piety, Directing a Christian how to walk with God*, 12th ed. (London, 1620), pp. 564, 594.

having been in much trouble of mind about her spiritual estate, at length grew into utter desperation, and could not endure to hear of any comfort, &c., so as one day she took her little infant and threw it into a well and then came into the house and said, now she was sure she should be damned for she had drowned her child."[3] Puritan autobiographies, which chronicle the writers' attempts to determine their spiritual status, record long periods of self-loathing and despair.[4]

Responding to the disturbing implications of such a conception of the human condition, Puritan men found in Paul a metaphorical understanding of gender relations by which to deflect their own ambivalence about Original Sin onto women. Paul's analogy that man corresponds to woman as head to body or spirit to flesh provides a "logic" by which male believers can resolve their own feelings of insecurity and self-contempt. To lay the foundation for my discussion of Puritan literature, I offer here a discussion of how the Pauline metaphysics of gender operates in the Epistles and in Puritan sermons and treatises. Because Puritan ministers and domestic theorists based their understanding of marital and familial relationships on an unreconstructed, literal reading of the Pauline epistles and the New Testament household codes, I will not attempt to suggest positive ways in which the Epistles might be interpreted today but will employ what Elisabeth Schussler Fiorenza calls a feminist "hermeneutics of suspicion," recognizing that "certain texts of the Bible can be used against women's struggles for liberation not only because they are patriarchally misinterpreted but because they are patriarchal texts and therefore serve to legitimate women's subordinate role and secondary status in patriarchal society and church."[5]

3. John Winthrop, *The History of New England from 1630–1649, from his original manuscripts*, ed. James Savage (Boston: Phelps and Farnham, Printer, 1825), 1:236.

4. Some influential examples include Richard Baxter, *The Breviate Life of Margaret Charlton* (1681); John Bunyan, *Grace Abounding to the Chief of Sinners* (1666); Jonathan Edwards, *Personal Narrative* (1739) and *Of the Surprising Conversions* (1737).

5. Elisabeth Schussler Fiorenza, *Bread Not Stone: The Challenge of Feminist Biblical Interpretation* (Boston: Beacon Press, 1984), p. xii.

Puritanism inherited from the Apostle Paul its most complete expression of the paradoxical quality of human nature: "But I see another law in my members, warring against the law of my mind, and bringing me into captivity to the law of sin which is in my members. O wretched man that I am! who shall deliver me from the body of this death?" (Rom. 7:23–24).[6] Paul describes unregenerate human nature as hopelessly corrupt, because the Law exposes rather than protects from sin. Only in the act of faith does the unrighteous become justified and sanctified. But while Paul preaches that the believer will "put on the new man, which after God is created in righteousness and true holiness" (Eph. 4:24), and that "unto the pure all things are pure" (Tit. 1:15), he qualifies these assertions with warnings that anticipate and seek to prevent the idea that the saved soul is above the Law or that all its impulses will be holy and pure: "What, then? shall we sin, because we are not under the law, but under grace? God forbid" (Rom. 6:15). The regenerate Christian is still capable of sin and responsible for moral choice.

Paul insists that the Gospel offers freedom from, not freedom for, the flesh—"For, brethren, ye have been called unto liberty, only use not liberty for an occasion to the flesh" (Gal. 5:13)—and advises controlling fleshly desires, for one's own sake and as an example to others: "All things are lawful unto me, but all things are not expedient: all things are lawful for me, but I will not be brought under the power of any" (1 Cor. 6:12). This passage, addressing the problem of fornication among a congregation of the saved, acknowledges that the struggle against fleshly desires does not end by justification in Christ. As Paul exhorts his congregation, "Know ye not that your bodies are the members of Christ? shall I then take the members of Christ and make them the members of a harlot? God forbid" (1 Cor. 6:15). In this context, the famous declaration "Know ye not that your body is the temple of the Holy Ghost which is in you, which ye have of God" (1 Cor. 6:19) does not offer an unambiguous glori-

6. Although modern New Testament scholars accept only 1 Thessalonians, Galatians, 1 and 2 Corinthians, Romans, Philippians, and Philemon as authentically Paul's, I will conform to Puritan belief and practice, treating all the epistles attributed to Paul in the New Testament as his.

fication of the body. Instead, the struggle between the motions of the spirit and the desires of the flesh offers the testing ground for a Christian's commitment: "For the flesh lusteth against the Spirit, and the Spirit against the flesh" (Gal. 5:17). The body, like a temple, can be desecrated as well as sanctified.

In Pauline thought, the body that a couple becomes in marriage takes its place within a definitive hierarchy of capacity as well as status: "But I would have you know, that the head of every man is Christ; the head of the woman is the man; and the head of Christ is God" (1 Cor. 11:3). Paul clings to patriarchy and the old order even as he proclaims a new one, interpreting the subordination of woman to man as a natural or innocent condition, exaggerated but not instituted by the Fall. His visionary proclamations about a genderless life in the Spirit coexist with his proscriptions about the place of women in the church. Paul divorces the idea of spiritual equality from his treatment of the real men and women in his congregation. While the precarious existence of the early Christian church and the supposedly imminent Second Coming to some extent motivate Paul's conservative counsel regarding both marriage and slavery (see Col. 3:22, 1 Tim. 6:1–2, 1 Cor. 7:20–22), neither an expectation of Apocalypse nor concern about survival in a hostile, conservative society can wholly explain his failure to admit women into the church as fully enfranchised members.[7]

Paul's vision of the spiritual equality of believers is logically inconsistent with his strictures about the participation of women in the church. He claims that in the spiritual realm "there is neither Jew nor Greek, there is neither bond nor free, there is neither male nor female: for ye are all one in Christ Jesus" (Gal. 3:28). Such a doctrine followed to its logical conclu-

7. For a discussion of the Aristotelian origins of the household code texts and their role as "an attempt to mitigate the subversive impact of religious conversion on the patriarchal order of house and of society," see Fiorenza, *Bread Not Stone*, pp. 70–80. For an exploration of evidence in support of an active egalitarian ministry in the church of the first two centuries, see Fiorenza, "Word, Spirit, and Power: Women in Early Christian Communities," in *Women of Spirit: Female Leadership in the Jewish and Christian Traditions*, ed. Rosemary Radford Ruether and Eleanor McLaughlin (New York: Simon and Schuster, 1977), pp. 30–70.

sion prohibits dividing the gifts of the spirit according to physical categories. On the issues of slavery and ethnic origin, Paul is consistent: no evidence in the epistles suggests that such spiritual gifts as prophesying, preaching, or teaching were divided according to social status. Nevertheless, Paul forbids women to speak in church or to exercise spiritual gifts (see 1 Cor. 14:34–35, 1 Tim. 2:11–12). Significantly, in 1 Corinthians Paul omits women from his proclamation of the democracy of believers: "For by one Spirit are we all baptized into one body, whether we be Jews or Gentiles, whether we be bond or free" (1 Cor. 12:13). Women, by contrast, are permanently excluded "Gentiles," permitted to enter the community only as secondary, silent members.

Both distrust of the flesh and an identification of the flesh with women contribute to Paul's defense of physical hierarchy within the church of the Spirit. I do not intend to psychoanalyze Paul or to suggest that this attitude toward women originates with him, for it clearly derives from more ancient sources. But Paul's subordination of women within marriage and the church because of their physical nature authorizes this devaluation of women and codifies it as an integral part of his gospel. While men have the flexibility to be both spiritual and physical, authoritative and subordinate—the "head," or representative of God, within the couple and the body, or "member of Christ," within the church—women become ontologically and essentially identified with "body." Although Paul is not contemptuous of the body in its gracious state, the way that a body becomes gracious is by subordinating itself to a head. A woman becomes gracious only through the marital relation: "Wives, submit yourselves to your husbands, as unto the Lord. For the husband is the head of the wife, even as Christ is the head of the Church: and he is the saviour of the body. Therefore as the church is subject unto Christ, so let the wives be to their own husbands in every thing" (Eph. 5:22–24). A man who becomes gracious by subordinating himself to Christ achieves through that self-denial both the opportunity to exercise power and authority within the church and the ability to identify himself with Christ as "head" of his family.

Relying wholly on masculine terms for God and for the believer, the Pauline epistles provide a vision of positive mas-
culinity, while offering no such image of the female. When Paul
advises, in the previously mentioned passage from 1 Corinthians, that the Gospel offers freedom from, not freedom for,
the flesh, he uses an example that equates flesh with female:
"Know ye not that your bodies are the members of Christ? shall
I then take the members of Christ, and make them the members of a harlot? God forbid" (1 Cor. 6:15). Paul again identifies
flesh with woman when he testifies to the significance of
Christ's incarnation: "But when the fulness of the time was
come, God sent forth his Son, made of a woman, made under
the law, To redeem them that were under the law, that we
might receive the adoption of sons." (Gal. 4:4–5). In this passage, the mother of Jesus becomes not an image of miraculous
and divine maternity but an embodiment of flesh under the
Law. To make clear the distinction between the old and new
covenants, Paul emphasizes not her virgin purity or unique role
as the bride of God but her participation in sinful humanity.
Through the intervention of Christ, believers transcend the
sinfulness associated with the female body, becoming spiritual
creatures, asexual "sons." They are not born "after the flesh"
but born again spiritually by the labor of male ministers and
apostles.

William Ames, formulating the Puritan interpretation of the
Incarnation in *The Marrow of Theology* (1629), follows Paul in
demystifying the Virgin Mary. He describes Mary's role as passive and nonredemptive: "She did nothing of herself—except to
provide the material out of which Christ was formed. Even for
that she could not immediately provide fit material (for hers
was not pure); it was made fit by a certain supernatural preparation and sanctification." Mary is not chosen because worthy
but worthy because chosen; except as an example of female
obedience and submission, her existence hardly signifies. Ames
explains that Christ has two distinct "sonships," a true relation
to God because of his "person" and a temporal relation to Mary
because "there is a relation of his human nature to his person
and of Mary to his human nature." In orthodox Puritan terms,

Ames reduces her motherhood to a purely biological function. Mary becomes Eve, not in the typological sense in which Christ is the antitype, or the second Adam, but through the identity of function: as Eve, in Ames's theology, is a secondary cause in the Fall, the instrument by which Adam fell, Mary becomes a secondary cause in the Incarnation, the medium through which the Son can take on sinful humanity. Significantly, Ames considers the moment of true union between the divine and human aspects of Christ to be not the Incarnation but the Ascension— not his birth into biological sonship but his adoption into spiritual sonship.[8]

Motherhood as Paul sets it forth in his epistles is thus not a gracious activity in which saved women exercise their gifts; instead, it places women under the old covenant of works as they participate in the fallen procreation of Eve and her Old Testament daughters. Paul interprets the Old Testament story of Hagar and Sarah typologically, as an allegory of the two covenants: Abraham's children by Hagar are his heirs "after the flesh," but his children by Sarah are his "children of the promise" (Gal. 4:22-31). As Martin Luther points out in his *Lectures on Galatians* (1535), Paul's reading of the Genesis story subordinates questions about the legitimacy and ethnic origin of the children to the freedom of God's choice: "The difference, Paul says, is not that one mother was a free woman and the other a slave—although this does contribute to the allegory—but that Ishmael, who was born of the slave, was born according to the flesh, that is, apart from the promise and the Word of God, while Isaac was not only born of the free woman but also in accordance with a promise."[9] According to Paul's analogy be-

---

8. William Ames, *The Marrow of Theology*, trans. from the 3d Latin ed. (1625) and ed. John D. Eusden (Durham, N.C.: Labyrinth Press, 1968), pp. 137, 138, 115-16. Ames writes, "This was an ascension of the whole person, but it belongs to the divine nature only figuratively. The divine nature is now joined to the human nature in sublimity and serves as the cause of the ascension— manifesting its glory, once emptied, as it were, when it entered into human nature at the incarnation. The ascension most properly applies to the human nature because it involved a change from a lower place to a higher" (pp. 146-47).

9. *Luther's Works*, ed. Jaroslav Pelikan, 55 vols. (St. Louis: Concordia, 1963), 26:434.

tween conversion and adoption, God through Christ acknowledges, or adopts, a believer, who becomes "no more a servant,
but a son" (Gal. 4:7), for "if ye be Christ's, then are ye Abraham's seed, and heirs according to the promise" (Gal. 3:29).
Fatherhood, in Judaic tradition, transcends biological necessity:
a man is the father of those children whom he chooses to
acknowledge, whereas motherhood is a purely biological condition. During the Jewish ceremony of circumcision, the father
names the son, thereby acknowledging him and accepting him
into the faith. Sigmund Freud, writing a secular history of this
tradition in *Moses and Monotheism*, suggests that the idea of
paternity arose concurrently with the idea of an invisible God.
Both concepts, he argues, herald "a victory of spirituality over
the senses" and are hallmarks of civilization, "since maternity
is proved by the senses whereas paternity is a surmise."[10] In the
spiritual realm, the man becomes both parents, and all children
are sons.

   Throughout his epistles, Paul argues against circumcision
because Christ's sacrifice fulfilled the Law and made it void,
"for by the works of the law shall no flesh be justified" (Gal.
2:16). But according to Paul's interpretation, the terms of the
new covenant do not apply equally to women. Paul and his
school consistently reveal an inability to dissociate a woman's
self from her physical body; the most explicit expression of this
identification comes in 1 Timothy: "But I suffer not a woman to
teach, nor to usurp authority over the man, but to be in silence.
For Adam was first formed, then Eve. And Adam was not deceived, but the woman being deceived was in the transgression.
Notwithstanding she shall be saved in childbearing, if they
continue in faith and charity and holiness with sobriety" (1
Tim. 2:14–15). This passage suggests that a woman's spiritual
security depends on her physical productivity. Such thinking
contradicts Paul's assertion that believers are saved by faith in
Christ, rather than by works. The passage also asserts that the
biological fact of gender influences a person's relationship to
grace, emphasizing a woman's subordinate status within mar-

---

10. Sigmund Freud, *Moses and Monotheism*, trans. Katherine Jones (New
York: Vintage Press, 1967), p. 145.

riage and the family. It places women in the same category as unbelievers married to believers, as individuals who may be sanctified by association despite spiritual incapacity (see 1 Cor. 7:12–16). Salvation through authorized childbearing identifies a woman's physical with her spiritual condition; it allows the categories of the flesh to intrude upon the realm of the spirit.

To Puritans, who believed rigorously in justification by faith alone, this passage presented serious theological difficulties. Richard Adams, a Puritan clergyman who discussed this text at the Morning-Exercises at Cripplegate in 1682, addresses the problem bluntly: "But how can child-bearing, which is a natural thing, either affect or deserve eternal salvation?" Adams argues that childbearing is not the cause but *"the ordinary way wherein* pious wives, apt to be suspicious and fearful, should meet with saving help from God, who would lead them on therein to salvation." He suggests that pregnancy constitutes "an affliction," a test imposed on women by God as the appropriate forum for their exercise of such Christian virtues as patience, submission, and obedience. If pregnant women conduct themselves appropriately under the affliction of their condition, then "the pains shall be sanctified, and be no obstacle to their welfare; their souls shall be safely delivered."[11] In *Elizabeth in her Holy Retirement* (Boston, 1710), Cotton Mather subordinates the danger of the physical birth to the urgency of the spiritual one, exclaiming, "You have a *Child formed in you.* But, Oh! That you might have a CHRIST *formed in you!*" He warns the pregnant woman: "For ought you know, your *Death* has entred into you, and you may have conceived That which determines but about Nine Months more at the most, for you to Live in the World"; if she does not take this opportunity to repent of her sins and accept Christ as her savior, "the *Sorrows* of *Child-birth* will be to you, but the *Beginning of Sorrows*, and of such as know no *End.*"[12]

11. Richard Adams, "How may child-bearing women be most encouraged and supported against, in, and under the hazard of their travail?" in *Puritan Sermons, 1659–1689* (Wheaton, Ill.: Robert Owen Roberts, 1981), pp. 534, 537, 532.

12. Cotton Mather, *Elizabeth in her holy Retirement,* (Evans American Bibliography, Catalogue #1463), pp. 20, 6, hereafter cited in the text by page number.

Mather's grim warning represents an attitude toward pregnancy foreign to modern sensibilities. In our experience, childbirth is not a life-threatening condition. In the United States in
1981, only 8.5 out of every 100,000 live births resulted in the
death of the mother.[13] But while the statistics for the seventeenth century are hard to confirm because church registers
reported the fact but not the cause of death, historians agree
that in colonial New England, one out of every thirty births
caused the death of the mother. In other words, one out of five
women died of complications resulting from childbirth. Because about three out of ten children died in infancy and the
average colonial wife had six to eight children, she could also
expect to lose at least one child. In Europe, where overcrowding
and poor sanitation created greater health risks, these statistics
were slightly worse. There is no conclusive evidence about how
many pregnancies might end in miscarriage, but Lawrence
Stone suggests that a conservative estimate would be between 4
and 10 percent. Catherine Scholten notes that women frequently received serious, irreparable injuries during childbirth, such
as "tears of the bladder, rectum, and vagina." She also reminds
us that fear of death in childbirth would be "magnified in small
communities by intimate knowledge of the circumstances" of
other women's deaths.[14]

Puritan clergymen considered pregnancy the appropriate sea-
son during which to exhort a woman to repent and be saved, not
simply because the woman might die during labor but because
the particular circumstances of pregnancy should convince a
woman of her horrible sinfulness. Mather argues that "the Hazards and Hardships undergone by the Travailing Daughters of

13. U.S. Census Bureau, *Statistical Abstracts of the United States, 1985,*
105th ed. (Washington, D.C.: Government Printing Office, 1984), table 108, p.
73.
14. Catherine Scholten, *Childbearing in American Society, 1650–1850*
(New York: New York University Press, 1985), p. 22. For bibliography and
further discussion of these statistics, see Lawrence Stone, *The Family, Sex, and
Marriage in England, 1500–1800* (New York: Harper and Row, 1977); Peter
Gregg Slater, *Children in the New England Mind in Death and Life* (Hampden,
Conn.: Archon, 1977); John Demos, *A Little Commonwealth: Family Life in
Plymouth Colony* (New York: Oxford University Press, 1970).

Eve, make a Considerable Article of the *Curse*, which the *Transgression* where-into she was *Deceived*, has brought upon the miserable World" (2). He informs the pregnant woman that "the *Griefs* which you are now suffering in your Body, are the Fruit of Sin," charging her to "think on that Word; Jam. I.15. *When Lust hath conceived, it brings forth Sin, and sin when it is finished, brings forth Death*" (18). In *A Present for Teeming Women* (London, 1663), John Oliver encourages the pregnant woman to meditate on "this unsightly act of generation," voicing her probable response as "Alas, how vile are those materials of which my body was made. . . . My *vile body*? In nothing so vile, than in its first coagulation of ignoble matter."[15] In a system of metaphor in which sexuality stands for sinfulness, the contemplation of conception leads inevitably to conviction of sin.

Puritan clergymen exploit this connection between sexuality and sin, drawing their metaphors for the woman's spiritual crisis from her experience of pregnancy. Mather relates, "Some Women that have been in *Horror of Conscience*, have declared, that all the Anguish of bringing more than Seven Children into the World has been much more tolerable, than that horrible Anguish of their Mind" (8), while Oliver draws an elaborate analogy between the woman's physical peril and her greater spiritual danger: "While you carry a burthen in your wombs, then, if ever, you had need to be eased of the heavier burthen of sin, which cannot be done without repentance. You must repent of the miscarriages of your lives, if you would be provided against the danger of a miscarrying womb. You must willingly endure the pangs of repentance, if you would safely bear the pangs of your travel" (43). Oliver warns, however, that physical deliverance cannot be interpreted as evidence of spiritual grace, for "*if they be delivered* while yet they retain such unwillingness of mind to prepare for death, (as we say of all other deliverance granted the ungodly) they are delivered *in anger not in*

---

15. Quotations are from the 2d ed. of John Oliver's pamphlet, called *A Present to be given to Teeming Women* (London, 1669), pp. 63, 64, courtesy of the Burke Library of Union Theological Seminary, hereafter cited in the text by page number.

favour, with God's curse not with his blessing, and are (in all likelyhood) reserved to the greater condemnation when their *Sin is Ripened"* (Preface). Similarly, an incomplete repentance threatens a woman's hope of salvation. Mather exhorts his congregation to "be as much afraid of Leaving any Sin unconfessed, as you would be of having the *After-birth left in you,* after your Travail" (9). Convinced of her sinfulness, the pregnant woman should be moved to pray with Paul that she might have a "safe and happy deliverance from *this body of death"* (Oliver, 69). Like Mather, Oliver urges women to "fly to Christ for refuge, then they are safe; for whether they live or die their souls cannot miscarry" (Preface). As the breach of the old covenant exposed women to the pain and danger of childbirth, so the observation of the new covenant will preserve them from it, not necessarily with physical deliverance but with spiritual salvation.

According to these ministers, an appropriate response to pregnancy means cheerful submission to the will of God and to biology. Recognizing that "the will of the Great God, has been declared in these Terms, I Tim. V.14 *I will that the Younger Women, Marry, bear Children"* (Mather, 3–4), the pious wife could neither lament her condition nor desire to avoid future pregnancies. Mather warns his readers against being *"Dissatisfied* at your State of *Pregnancy. Froward Pangs of Dissatisfaction* harboured, and humoured, in you, because you See that *in Sorrow you are to bring forth Children,* may displease Heaven, and bring yet more *Sorrow* upon you" (3). Each of these clergymen invokes that "Gracious *Promise* of God unto His People, *That they should have an Offspring"* (Mather, 4), a promise that extends to "all the seed of *Abraham* (I mean, that continue in the faith of *Abraham)"* (Oliver, 4). Because, under covenant theology, the children of church members would qualify for baptism and church membership, those church members ought to feel the responsibility to reproduce "that God might have *holy seed"* (Oliver, 2). The believing mother who yields to God's will brings forth at her delivery two offspring of Christ, her own soul and a new member of the church covenant.

Although Puritans interpreted the community of the covenant spiritually, as in Paul's declaration that "if ye be Christ's, then are ye Abraham's seed, and heirs according to the promise" (Gal. 3:29), they believed that children of believers were more likely than others to become those heirs. While the innkeeper Gaius in *The Pilgrim's Progress* defines Christian's family as the community of Christian martyrs, he nonetheless encourages Christiana to marry off Christian's physical sons, "that the name of their father and the house of his progenitors may never be forgotten."[16] Both Mather and Adams praise the determination of Elizabeth Joceline, author of *A Mother's Legacy* (Oxford, 1684), to produce a new member for the church. They point out that, although she "had a Strong presage, which prov'd a True One, of her *Dying* by her Travail, yet you read in her *Legacy* Written for her unborn Child, her *Desire of God, that she might be a Mother to One of His Children*" (Mather, 5). They encourage women to emulate her. They also offer as models biblical women who died in childbirth, such as Rachel and the wife of Phinehas, and pregnant women who submitted themselves graciously to God's will, such as Sarah, Elizabeth, and Mary. They remind women of Paul's assurance: "*Notwithstanding her sin,* God will save her; *notwithstanding the curse,* God will bless her" (Oliver, 137).[17]

II

As careful students of the Pauline epistles, Puritan divines followed Paul's precedent in restricting the powers and privileges of women within their churches. They, too, treated women as second-class believers, supporting their arguments about female inferiority with the analogy that the man is the head, the woman the body. Indeed, the strength of the Puritan

16. John Bunyan, *The Pilgrim's Progress,* ed. Roger Sharrock (New York: Penguin Books, 1965), p. 315, hereafter cited in the text by page number.

17. In *Elizabeth in Her Holy Retirement,* Mather offers women more than legalistic assurance: when a woman accepts Christ as her savior, the baby in her womb becomes his child, "a *Member* of His Mystical Body." She is "made a Wife unto Salvation," a Bride of Christ in this life.

attack on female participation seems to reflect a political situation within the dissenting community similar to that identified
by historical reconstructionists in the early Christian church:
female believers, interpreting the Gospel as preaching a disci-
pleship of equals, exercised their spiritual gifts and claimed
authority to teach and preach the Gospel; hierarchically conservative groups reacted vehemently to protect male ecclesiastical
authority.[18] In his study of radical religious movements among
the laboring and itinerant classes, Christopher Hill records nu-
merous instances in which both men and women claimed the
spiritual and social equality of the sexes on Pauline grounds.[19]
The pamphlet of Quaker leader Margaret Askew Fell Fox,
Womens Speaking Justified (London, 1667), offers a fine example of the ability of seventeenth-century women to expose the
biased applications of Pauline material to female participation
in church. The brutal punishment of Quaker women who dared
to speak with authority in public and in the churches, however,
witnesses to the inflexibility of the established clergy, Puritan
and Anglican alike. Elaine C. Huber also documents a conservative trend within the Quaker community during its first fifty
years which ultimately led to restricted roles for women.[20] Like
her Quaker counterparts, the antinomian Ann Hutchinson led
Bible study groups, unsupervised by men, and for her claims to
prophetic authority and divine revelation, she was excommuni-
cated and expelled from Massachusetts Bay.[21]

   A desire to conform completely and literally to early church
practice as conveyed by the Pauline epistles informs Puritan
discussion of church proceedings, especially in relation to

    18. See Elisabeth Schussler Fiorenza, "The Will to Choose or Reject: Con-
tinuing Our Critical Work," in *Feminist Interpretation of the Bible*, ed. Letty
M. Russell (Philadelphia: Westminster Press, 1985), p. 134.
    19. Christopher Hill, *The World Turned Upside Down: Radical Ideas during
the English Revolution* (London: Temple Smith, 1972).
    20. Elaine C. Huber, "A Woman Must Not Speak: Quaker Women in the
English Left Wing" in *Women of Spirit*, pp. 154–81.
    21. See both the record of her trial and the report to the church at Boston on
that trial in David Hall, ed., *The Antinomian Controversy, 1636–1638: A
Documentary History* (Middletown, Conn.: Wesleyan University Press, 1968),
pp. 311–88.

women's participation. Bunyan insists throughout *A Case of Conscience Resolved* that he objects to separate women's prayer meetings because he can find no New Testament precedent. Bunyan informs the offending women that "the Holy Ghost doth particularly insist upon the inability of women, as to their well-managing of the worship *now* under consideration." To secure his point, he appeals to the marital relation: "If this worship may be managed by the sisterhood of the churches, being congregated together in the absence of their men: of what signification is it that man is the head of the women as well in worship as in nature?" Bunyan reconciles this belief with Paul's statement that in Christ there is neither male nor female by distinguishing between the visible and the invisible church. Bunyan applies "neither male nor female" to "that church which is his true mystical body, and not of every particular congregation of professing Christians." He promises the women in his congregation that "this inferiority of yours will last but a little while." At the Last Judgment, "these distinctions of sexes shall be laid aside. . . . For with a *notwithstanding* you shall be saved." Alluding to Paul's arguments in 1 Timothy about the natural and spiritual inferiority of women, Bunyan emphasizes their secondary status, even within the covenant of grace. Eve's disobedience "overthrew, as to that, the reputation of women forever." Bunyan concludes his remarks with a disclaimer that defines a good woman as one who assents to his argument: "Nor do I think, that any woman that is holy and humble, will take offense at what I have said; for I have not in anything sought to degrade them, or to take from them what either nature or grace, or an appointment of God hath invested them with: but have laboured to keep them in their place."[22] In a world that defines a hierarchy of worth and ability according to gender as natural and inevitable, dialogue becomes impossible.

Similarly, in *Singing of Psalms a Gospel-Ordinance* (1650),

---

22. John Bunyan, *A Case of Conscience Resolved*, in *The Works of John Bunyan*, ed. George Offor, 3 vols. (Glasgow: Blackie, 1856), 2:662–63, 664, 665, 671, 672, 664, 674.

John Cotton uses the Pauline epistles to defend the practice of allowing women to join in public psalm singing. Under the heading "Concerning the singers: whether women, pagans, and profane or carnal persons," Cotton dismisses the idea that psalm singing constitutes speaking in church. He argues that women should join the singing, even though Paul forbids them to speak in church (1 Cor. 13:34, 1 Tim. 2:11–12), because such supervised singing cannot be construed as either teaching, questioning, or prophesying. Someone else has decided what is to be sung; the women, in singing along, simply assent. Cotton acknowledges a Pauline precedent when he appeals to the Law, pointing to Old Testament examples of women who sang praise. The apostle, he asserts, "requireth the *same* subjection in the women which the *Law* had put upon them—*no more.*" While the Gospel frees men from the constraints of the Law, it simply protects women from additional subjugation. If Cotton's defense of women's participation suggests that he held more liberal views than some of his Puritan contemporaries, his position on "pagans, and profane or carnal persons" raises some doubts: "It is a further glory to God that such Pagans and profane persons should sing the word of God to their own conviction and confusion of face."[23] Singing psalms is not a privileged form of worship: it is a duty, exacted of believer and nonbeliever alike.

The same terms that govern discussions of public worship apply to family worship as well. In *Of Domesticall Duties* (1622), William Gouge charges husbands to attend to their wives' religious education, explaining their responsibility to "nourish and cherish [their wives], not only as their bodies, but as Christ nourisheth and cherisheth his Church, not only with things temporall, but also with things spirituall and eternall." Gouge stresses the importance of family prayer as a mutual duty, but one that "doth especially concerne the husband, who

23. John Cotton, *Singing of Psalms a Gospel-Ordinance*, in *A Library of American Literature from the Earliest Settlement to the Present Time*, comp. and ed. Edmund Clarence Stedman and Ellen Mackay Hutchinson, 11 vols. (New York: Charles L. Webster, 1891), 1:254–70, quotations p. 267, emphasis mine.

is as a Priest unto his wife, and ought to be her mouth to God
when they two are together."[24] Bunyan strengthens this point
with an analogy between women and angels, which he draws in
part from Hebrews: "As the angels in heaven are not Christ, and
so not admitted to the mercy-seat to speak to God, so neither
are women on earth, [but] the man; who is to worship with open
face before him, and be the mouth of prayer for the rest."[25]
Gouge defines the purpose of a husband's being "the head of his
wife, namely that by his provident care he may be as a saviour to
her" (30). Such an analogical understanding of human relations
reinforces woman's inferiority—which is the first point Gouge
addresses in the treatise—as both natural and necessary within
a universal hierarchy; at the same time it offers men an external
scapegoat to blame for their own lusts and onto whom to project their self-contempt. Not only are women inferior by nature,
but their subjection is also a punishment for Eve's role in the
Fall. Gouge warns from biblical precedent against female independence and dominance, urging that "she who first drew man
into sin should be now subject to him, lest by like womanish
weaknesse she fall again" (267).

This tendency to dismiss women as spiritually incapable
flourished in English society, Separating or Non-Separating,
throughout the seventeenth century. The Anglican Jeremy Taylor describes Christ's mystical marriage with the church in
language that espouses the identification of divinity and the
soul with man, of flesh and blood with woman. Defining for a
newly united couple the wife's duty to obey her husband, he
asks incredulously "if the body shall give laws, and, by the
violence of the appetite, first abuse the understanding, and then
possess the superior portion of the will and choice[?]" Significantly, when Taylor wishes to praise marriage and the companionship it provides, he writes, "For a good woman is in her soul
the same that a man is, and she is a woman only in her body;

24. William Gouge, *Of Domesticall Duties* (London, 1622), reproduced from
the Bodleian Library copy (Amsterdam: Theatrum Orbis Terrarum, 1976), pp.
79, 235, hereafter cited in the text by page number.
25. Bunyan, *Case of Conscience*, 2:672. The bracketed "but" was inserted by
the editor.

that she may have the excellency of the one, and the usefulness of the other, and become amiable in both."[26] In Christ there is neither male nor female, it seems, not because in the spirit the sexes achieve equality of ability, value, and privilege, not even because in the spirit biological distinctions become irrelevant, but because in the spirit there is only male: "She is a woman only in her body."

Puritan women quite naturally use marital typology to describe their own spiritual situations. Anne Bradstreet comforts herself for the loss of her bridal home in "Some Verses upon the Burning of Our House. July 10th, 1666," by remembering that she has a better house and a spiritual bridegroom in heaven.[27] John Winthrop employs the same symbolism to console his wife in his absence: "If now Christ be thy Husband, thou must show what sure and sweet intercourse is between him and thy soul, when it shall be no hard thing for thee to part with an earthly, mortal, infirm husband for his sake."[28] But when the realities of women's experience are spiritualized to create metaphors for male spirituality, the actual earthly activities of childbirth and mothering become devalued.

In comparing the relationship of a husband to his wife with that of Christ to the Church or to the individual believer, Paul indicates a pattern, adopted later as a structural device by male Christian writers, in which the earthly roles of women are usurped as symbolic spiritual stances by males. In Romans 7:1–6, Paul compares the converted soul to a woman who, because her husband (the Law) has died, is free to marry another (Christ). Jeremy Taylor explains in a sermon of 1653 that "Christ descended from his Father's bosom, and contracted his divinity with flesh and blood, and married our nature, and we became a church, the spouse of the Bridegroom, which he cleansed with his blood, and gave her his Holy Spirit for a dowry, and heaven

26. In *The Whole Works of the Right Reverend Jeremy Taylor, D.D.*, ed. Reginald Heber, 15 vols. (London: Ogle, Duncan, 1822), 5:273, 252.

27. In *The Works of Anne Bradstreet*, ed. Jeannine Hensley (Cambridge: Belknap Press of Harvard University, 1967).

28. John Winthrop to his wife, Jan. 31, 1629, in *Library of American Literature*, 1:308.

for a jointure; begetting children unto God by the Gospel."[29] Similarly, Paul appropriates motherhood as a metaphor for his relationship to his congregation, writing to the Galatians, "I travail in birth again until Christ be formed in you" (Gal. 4:19). In his preface to *Grace Abounding* (1666), Bunyan describes himself as the mother of his congregation.[30] In *A Present for Teeming Women*, Oliver casts human ministers in the role of midwives and travailing mothers. The female speaker in Oliver's sample meditation on that passage laments, "Like those inconstant Galatians, I have caused [my minister] again and again to travel with me in birth." She recognizes that it would be just in Old Testament terms were "God to plague me with a tedious, painful, and fruitless travel" but concludes more hopefully that her labor may go well "if God thus bless and answer him in his prayers and travel for the new birth of my soul" (74–75). The minister's spiritual labor will assist both the spiritual and the physical birth. The soul becomes the true Bride, of which earthly women are but inferior copies; the apostle, evangelist, or minister becomes the spiritual mother, for which biological motherhood provides a convenient metaphor.

In his collection of emblematic poems *A Book For Boys and Girls* (1686), Bunyan combines Paul's analogical reading of the marital relation with biblical typology in a way that neatly and absolutely identifies man with spirit and woman with flesh. His poem "Of Moses and his Wife" teaches,

> This *Moses* was a fair and comely man;
> His wife a swarthy Ethiopian:
> Nor did his Milk-white Bosom change her Skin;
> She came out thence as black as she went in:
> Now *Moses* was a type of *Moses* Law,
> His Wife likewise of one that never saw
> Another way unto eternal Life;
> There's Myst'ry then in *Moses* and his wife.
>   The Law is very Holy, Just and good,
>   And to it is espous'd all Flesh and Blood:

29. Jeremy Taylor, "The Marriage-Ring; or, The Mysteriousness and Duties of Marriage," *Works*, 5:254.

30. John Bunyan, Preface to *Grace Abounding to the Chief of Sinners*, ed. Roger Sharrock (Oxford: Clarendon Press, 1962), pp. 1–4.

> But this its Goodness it cannot bestow,
> On any that are wedded thereunto.[31]

In the terms of the poem, Moses represents not man under the Law, as historically he was, but the Law itself; his wife takes his place as "flesh." Within their marriage, he embodies what is "Holy, Just, and good," while she remains "black" and unredeemed. As an educational comparison, Bunyan's analogy fulfils its purpose: we understand that the Law is nonredemptive. But just as the use of racial differences to illustrate spiritual difference reflects and perpetuates racist reality, the distance from Moses' marriage as an example of life under the Law to that marriage as a model for all marriages is disconcertingly small. According to Bunyan's understanding of marriage, the typological analogy between Moses' wife and sinful flesh rests upon human reality.

The companion poem to "Of Moses and his Wife" seems to offer a model of Christian or redemptive marriage. In "Of the Spouse of Christ," Bunyan relates how Christ raised the Church from ignominy to glory as his "Joynt-Heir." But the poem breaks awkwardly from rejoicing in the union into a direct warning to the Bride against overvaluing herself:

> Take heed of pride, remember what thou art,
> By Nature, tho thou hast in Grace a share:
> Thou in thy self doth yet retain a part
> Of thine own Filthiness, wherefore beware.[32]

Bunyan's warning against pride might be prudent were he addressing an individual believer, but in this context its tone seems wholly inappropriate. One simply does not say "Well, Lady, well, God has been good to thee" to the Invisible Church represented by an allegorical figure. Bunyan cannot seem to distinguish here between praising a female symbol and praising a real woman. He displaces his vehemence against women onto

---

31. John Bunyan, *The Poems*, ed. Graham Midgely (Oxford: Clarendon Press, 1980), p. 236.
32. Ibid. p. 259.

the church, systematically retracting his praise and reducing this lady—because she is female—back to her place of ignominy.

III

In order to offer believers a viable model for their own conduct in this world, Puritan authors present their positive characters not as abstract embodiments of ideas but as individuals capable of growing toward those virtues. In Puritan allegory, characters do not represent a Virtue or a Vice; they act virtuously or viciously: a Puritan allegorical character is Hopeful, not Speranza, or Mrs. Love-the-Flesh, not a personification of lust. As a Bunyan character in *Pilgrim's Progress* explains, "Not Honesty in the abstract, but Honest is my name, and I wish that my nature shall agree to what I am called" (300). Carolynn Van Dyke points out that even Spenser's Red Cross Knight, weighted down as he is with allegorical trappings, embodies "holiness only putatively and potentially."[33] Spenser wants to teach his reader how to be a gentleman, but he uses consciously archaic romance conventions as the vehicle for his instruction; he does not really expect the reader to buy a horse and go out "pricking on the plaine." But as Puritan literature becomes less aristocratic, a movement that occurs not simply chronologically from author to author but also within Milton's career, the situations in which the characters find themselves become more intimately related to the lives of their readers. When Bunyan presents his allegory of spiritual quest, he chooses his characters and episodes from working-class English life; when Milton offers an allegory of the willful self-destruction of sinfulness, he has Sin discuss her conflicting responsibilities to God and to Satan as if she were an ordinary Puritan housewife.

This desire to apply spiritual paradigms to ordinary experi-

---

33. Carolynn Van Dyke, *The Fiction of Truth: Structures of Meaning in Narrative and Dramatic Allegory* (Ithaca: Cornell University Press, 1985), p. 252, hereafter cited in the text by page number.

ence causes Puritan literature to teeter precariously on the
brink between allegory and realism. Indeed, in the Puritan
world, literary allegorical language and the language of everyday spiritual experience tend to become conflated. Bunyan's
characters talk the way Bunyan's readers talked; they interpret
their experiences the way readers interpreted their own lives.
As Van Dyke argues, Puritan allegorical figures, even those that
remain relatively static, are *capable* of ontological change and
are challenged, like real Puritans, to learn to read present human experience in terms of spiritual reality, to fuse "individual
experience and abstract truth" (186, 194–95). In *The Pilgrim's
Progress*, it is the task of the man clothed in rags to integrate
two orders of experience—to see earthly and spiritual reality as
one—so that, although he "is not simply mankind in the abstract, being differentiated to some degree from Faithful and
Hopeful," he can "appear, by metaphoric transformation, as the
syncretic, universal Christian" (189).

Not surprisingly, Van Dyke identifies in *Pilgrim's Progress*,
Part 2, an "internalization of metaphor . . . that leads from
allegory toward what we now call realism" (196), finding that
"the allegorical world is reconciled with the realistic one by
being absorbed into the thoughts, speech, and imaginations of
human beings" (194). In other words, transcendent external
realities become metaphors and analogies for psychological
conditions. At the close of Part 2, "the carnal world has assimi-
lated the allegorical one entirely" (197). This transformation in
the nature of the allegory in *The Pilgrim's Progress* coincides
with the introduction of women as protagonists. Van Dyke
argues that "to say that Part 2 is thus 'humanized' because it
concerns women and children is to forestall rather than offer an
explanation" (188). She subordinates the decision to include
women and children to a desire to avoid "tautology by differen-
tiating his new pilgrims from Christian and from each other as
fully as possible" (187). She claims that it is Christiana's status
as a "variant" of Christian that prevents her from achieving
that representativeness.

But I would argue that Part 2 is "humanized," or made carnal,
not through but because of its female protagonists. In *The Pil-*

grim's Progress, other male characters besides Christian have the potential, realized for example in Faithful's martyrdom, to achieve a metaphoric transformation into the representative Christian believer. Female characters, because they are women, do not. Christiana cannot represent universal Christian experience. As a secondary participant in the covenant of grace, she represents a variant of Christian that is essentially secondary, essentially different. Because Puritan theology insists on a woman's sexuality, her essential physicalness, Christiana's allegorical experience is absorbed into carnal reality. Mercy, "wife of Matthew," as "a young and breeding woman," cannot grow to embody her virtue. Women can only represent women in the confines of their social roles—as maidens, wives, mothers, whores. Those characterizations must be realistic, or they will fail to serve as either models or deterrents.

This assimilation of the allegorical world into the carnal also occurs in the course of Britomart's story in Book 3 of *The Faerie Queene*. Each of the Renaissance narratives I will discuss in this book is a derivative, or secondary, tale. The quests of Britomart and Christiana are literally derivative, each female story following and modeled on an earlier male story that determined the nature of the landscape and activity; the story of Eve is essentially so, for although *Paradise Lost* precedes *Paradise Regained* as a literary composition and as an historically located work, Milton builds into the structure of *Paradise Lost* the primacy of the Son's gracious obedience, so that his behavior during the Council in Heaven becomes a standard for Eve's prelapsarian marriage and a model for her postlapsarian efforts at reconciliation through self-sacrifice. Each of these women's stories is what Nancy Miller has defined in terms of the eighteenth-century novel as "the heroine's text . . . that codes femininity in the paradigms of sexual vulnerability" and moves toward a telos in marriage.[34] Each story ends with the woman's rejection of independent quest in favor of marital and social subordination.

---

34. Nancy K. Miller, *The Heroine's Text: Readings in the French and English Novel, 1722–1782* (New York: Columbia University Press, 1980), p. xi.

In his famous discussion of human nature in *Areopagitica,*
Milton declares, "Assuredly we bring not innocence into the
world, we bring impurity much rather: that which purifies us is
trial, and trial is by what is contrary."[35] He praises the trials of
"the true wayfaring Christian." The female equivalent of this
archetypal warrior-believer is the Bride of Christ, whose sufferings and wanderings are recorded in the Song of Solomon and
Revelations. But the idea of the Bride carries with it the idea of
innate purity and assumes a distinction between the sexually
charged outrages suffered by the body—the watchmen who tear
at her veil—and her spiritual integrity, between her intense
sexual longing and her moral innocence. While such Puritan
figures as Una, Christiana, and the Lady in *Comus* are all manifestations of the Bride motif, Puritan writers employ this para-
digm gingerly. Una remains allegorical, indeed becomes more
so as her story progresses, because she so explicitly represents
the True Church rather than a female believer; her sufferings
reflect not on her own spiritual inadequacies but on the failings
of her champion, the Red Cross Knight. But Christiana, because
she represents the individual female believer, dwindles from a
richly realized allegorical Bride of Christ in the opening of her
tale to a carnal figure, a "Mother in Israel." The bride of Christ
operates as a metaphor for the soul or the church but not as a
model for individual Christian women.[36]

Milton's treatment of the Lady in *Comus* offers an interesting
middle ground. Despite the claims her Elder Brother makes for
the supernatural quality of her chastity, the Lady is a representative character: she is a chaste woman, not Chastity itself.
In fact, Maryann McGuire defines her virtue as charity toward
God, arguing that "*Comus* offers the earliest and fullest poetic

35. John Milton, *Areopagitica,* in *The Complete Works of John Milton,* ed.
Frank Allen Paterson, 18 vols. (New York: Columbia University Press, 1931),
4:311. All further quotations from Milton's poetry and prose will be from the
Columbia Milton; the poetry will be noted by poem, book, and line number, the
prose by volume and page, in the text of my discussion, abbreviated *PL* for
Paradise Lost, PR for *Paradise Regained, W* for *Works, C* for *Comus.*

36. For an exception to this application of the metaphor, see Mather's *Elizabeth in her holy Retirement* and *Bethiah: The Glory which Adorns the Daughters of God* (Boston, 1722) Evans American Bibliography, Catalogue #2353.

development of the figure of spiritual marriage and the related motif of chastity as good works performed out of love of God."[37] McGuire places *Comus* in the context of the Recreation Controversy, a debate over the nature of Christian liberty sparked by the reissuance and proclamation of the *Declaration of Sports* in October 1633. Anglicans viewed Christian liberty as freedom to participate in "indifferent" activities, such as the ritual dancing and old English sports practiced by Comus's crew, while Puritans, following Paul's distinction—freedom *from*, not freedom *for* flesh—defined Christian liberty as "a freedom to work for the continuing edification of the Christian community."[38] As the Bride of Christ, the Lady resists the idolatrous, but also adulterous, temptation to put her own physical comfort and enjoyment before her obedience to God and concern for his community.

But the terms of her temptation and triumph are not wholly gender determined. The Lady is also a female "hero"; Milton allows her to exercise her virtue and to grow in moral awareness as a true wayfaring Christian. While Milton frames the Lady's adventure with the interventions of the Attendant Spirit, Sabrina, and her own ineffectual brothers, he focuses the plot on her moral test as an independent agent.[39] The Lady's heroism rests in her temperate resistance (she does not drink) not simply because she is female and therefore incapable of decisive action but because she is a *Puritan* hero exercising Christian liberty understood not as freedom from restraints "but as freedom to do all that is necessary to one's calling."[40] The Lady's passive resistance prefigures the ideal of post-Restoration Puritan literature. Heroism becomes a test not of physical activity or strength but of moral fortitude: a hero "stands."

37. Maryann McGuire, *Milton's Puritan Masque* (Athens: University of Georgia Press, 1983), p. 146.

38. Ibid., p. 28. For further discussion of the Puritan understanding of Christian liberty and edification, see Coolidge, *Pauline Renaissance*, pp. 23–54.

39. For a useful discussion of the distinction between the female heroine and the female hero, see the first chapter of Rachel Blau DuPlessis's *Writing beyond the Ending: Narrative Strategies of Twentieth-Century Women Writers* (Bloomington: Indiana University Press, 1985).

40. McGuire, *Milton's Puritan Masque*, p. 165.

Puritanism defines heroism as perseverance in loving obedience to God despite afflictions, a perseverance modeled on
Christ's sacrifice and the passive suffering of the early martyrs.
This conception of Christian heroism as suffering persecution
and afflictions for the Gospel began as early as the record in
Acts of the stoning of Stephen, whose challenge to his persecutors places his suffering in the context of earlier witnesses to
God's will: "Which of the prophets have not your fathers per-
secuted? and they have slain them which shewed before of the
coming of the Just One; of whom ye have been betrayers and
murderers" (Acts 7:52). Paul defines his own imitation of
Christ in terms of suffering and affliction; he bears on his body
the marks of his apostleship, the wounds he has received in
punishment for preaching the Gospel. As he understands the
world, "all that will live godly in Christ Jesus shall suffer persecution" (2 Tim. 3:12). Paul closes 2 Timothy, traditionally
believed to be the last letter he wrote from prison, with an
interpretation of his suffering as heroic: "For I am now ready to
be offered, and the time of my departure is at hand. I have fought
the good fight, I have finished my course, I have kept the faith"
(2 Tim. 4:6–7). Paul recognizes the truth of Jesus' claim that "ye
shall be hated of all men for my name's sake: but he that shall
endure unto the end, the same shall be saved" (Mark 13:13). He
has made himself ready to drink of Christ's cup and to be
baptized into his body through the spiritual baptism of crucifixion.

Milton structures both of his epic poems around this definition of heroism. In *Paradise Lost*, Abdiel, refusing to listen to
Satan's blasphemy, "Stood up, and in a flame of zeale severe /
The current of his fury thus oppos'd" (*PL* 5.807–8). He joins the
community of Christian martyrs who "for the testimonie of
truth [have] born / Universal reproach" (*PL* 6.32–33). In *Paradise
Regained*, Milton portrays Christ's victory over Satan's temptations as a calm, simple refusal: "To whom thus Jesus: also it is
written, / Tempt not the Lord thy God, he said and stood" (*PR*
4.560–61). These two moments suggest that heroism as standing comprises two elements: resisting temptation and witness-
ing to the truth. Abdiel denounces Satan although he is out-

numbered; he remains faithful "Among innumerable false, unmov'd, / Unshak'n, unseduc'd, unterrifi'd" (*PL* 5.898–99). On his return from the rebel camp, Abdiel receives the highest form of praise: "Servant of God, well done, well hast thou fought / The better fight" (*PL* 6.29–30). Bunyan, too, offers this solitary, nonviolent form of heroism. Christian leaves the City of Destruction despite protests and ridicule from his family and neighbors; Faithful, arrested for disturbing the peace in Vanity Fair, condemns that city's follies at the expense of his life.

These heroes redefine for themselves and their audience a heroism based on virtue rather than strength, on loyalty and obedience rather than on personal power. As Christ admonishes Satan,

> This is true glory and renown, when God,
> Looking on the earth, with approbation marks
> The just man.
> (*PR* 3.60–62)

Bunyan's Evangelist assures Christian and Faithful that "one or both of you must seal the testimony which you hold, with blood: but be you faithful unto death, and the King will give you a crown of life" (124). This kind of heroism is "the better fortitude / Of Patience and Heroic Martyrdom" (*PL* 9.31–32). The hero seeks divine, not human, approval; he wishes to be one in whom God is well pleased (Matt. 3:17, Mark 1:11, Luke 3:22).

These figures, reproached and reviled, "fearless, though alone, / Encompassed round with foes" (*PL* 5.875–76), exert a renewed appeal among dissenting Christians after the Restoration because they embody a heroism particularly suited to the frame of mind of the defeated party. With the Puritan revolution crushed, the Kingdom of God displaced by the kingdom of Charles II, Puritan authors worked to define a way to live within a secular society. They offer a model for Christian conduct in a hostile but prevailing world. Unlike John Foxe who, expecting the imminent arrival of the Kingdom, offered civil disobedience leading to martyrdom as the model of Christian sacrifice,[41]

41. See John Foxe, *The Acts and Monuments*, in *Foxe's Book of Martyrs*, ed. and abridged by G. A. Williamson (London: Secker and Warburg, 1965).

these latter-day Puritans stress quiet perseverance: they show how to stand and wait. Milton's God praises Abdiel, "for this was all thy care / To stand approved in sight of God" (*PL* 6.33–36).

But standing requires "sufficiency," an attribute that Puritan thinkers were reluctant to assign to women. As the subordinate half of the couple, the body rather than the head, a woman actually required male dominion. Paul defines subordination within the married couple as natural and necessary: "Neither was the man created for the woman; but the woman for the man" (1 Cor. 11:9); Puritan thinkers followed suit. Milton writes in *De Doctrina Christiana* that marriage was ordained at the creation as the "mutual love, society, help, and comfort of the husband and wife, though with a reservation of superior rights to the husband" (*W* 15.121).[42] His more famous statement of female subordination appears in *Paradise Lost*: "Hee for God only, shee for God in him" (*PL* 4.299). Although the prelapsarian relationship of Adam and Eve expresses a flexible mutuality, their conversations with one another, with God, and with the angel Raphael emphasize Adam's superior position within the marriage as guide and head. The Puritan theologian William Perkins defines a couple as two persons who, "standing in mutual relation to each other, are combined together as it were in one. And of these two the one is alwaies higher, and beareth rule, and the other is lower, and yeeldeth subjection."[43] Puritan writers stress this marital subordination as the only assurance of female virtue, pointing to female disobedience as the catalyst of the Fall. Milton argues that the first sin comprised "in the man excessive uxoriousness, in the woman a want of proper regard for her husband" (*W* 15.183). If a woman

42. Cf. Milton, *The Doctrine and Discipline of Divorce*, which, like the Puritan cases of conscience, recognizes that reality does not always conform to the ideal. There, Milton acknowledges that, if the wife surpasses her husband intellectually, then she might be "the head" in the marriage (*W* 3:475), although she must still be reverent.

43. William Perkins, *The Works of that famous and worthy minister of Christ in the Universitie of Cambridge, M. W. Perkins*, 3 vols. (Cambridge: Cantrell Legge, Printer to the Universitie of Cambridge, 1618), 3:670.

does not revere her husband, Gouge warns, "her nature will be more depraved, and her fault more increased" (268).

Eve, the weaker member of the couple-body, the disobedient wife, the original sinner, proves female frailty; her subsequent recognition of her own guilt, her repentance, and her submission to her husband's rule become the model for female virtue. A woman's virtue and spiritual security can be assured only through submission to male authority and reliance on male protection. Even the Lady in *Comus*, abandoned unwittingly by her brothers, must ultimately be rescued. The masque closes with a song that, though it replaces a wedding as the image of harmonious closure, predicts the Lady's future marriage. Puritanism offers no model for female celibacy. The Pauline statement that a woman would be saved through childbearing, combined with a belief that women require strict spiritual and moral supervision, mandates that women marry. Since woman's sphere is restricted to hearth and home, her *imitatio Christi*—her suffering and perseverance—can only take place within that environment.

The Puritan lying-in sermons present pregnancy as an occasion for heroic suffering; physical and emotional abuse, perversely, offered another. Elizabeth Ashbridge, a Quaker who wrote of her conversion, records how she suffered the mockery and cruelty of her husband and his friends because of her belief.[44] In Bunyan's *Life and Death of Mr. Badman* (1680), Mr. Badman's first wife, a "poor honest, and godly Damosel" whom he tricked into marriage, patiently endures his swearing, whoring, and drinking, disobeying him only by occasionally sneaking off to hear the Word preached. After her death, Mr. Wiseman relates, a second marriage teaches Mr. Badman the difference between a godly wife and a whore: "The first would be silent when he chid, and would take it patiently when he abused her, but this would give him word for word, blow for blow, curse for curse." On her deathbed, the first Mrs. Badman defines for her generation the heroism appropriate to a Christian woman: "I have

44. *The Journal of Elizabeth Ashbridge* (Philadelphia: Friends' Bookstore, [1808?]).

been a loving, faithful Wife unto thee; my prayers have been many for thee; and as for all the abuses that I have received at thy hand, those I freely and heartily forgive, and still shall pray for thy conversion, even as long as I breathe in this world." Her quiet, holy death prefigures that of Richardson's Clarissa. But despite her miserable circumstances and exemplary persever-ance, Mrs. Badman does not receive the sympathy of the men who tell her tale. Mr. Wiseman repeatedly reminds his listener that "now 'twas too late to repent, she should have looked better to herself, when being wary would have done her good." Because she was an orphan, she should have consulted her ministers and her religious friends about the match, rather "than to trust to her own poor, raw, womanish Judgment."[45] For these latter-day Puritans, female heroism is a condition for which there ought never to be an occasion; the heroine suffers her fate with the patient endurance of a victim who is responsi-ble for what she gets.[46]

IV

While I have undertaken in this book to trace the influence of a particular theological doctrine on several texts, my discussion is in no sense a comprehensive history of Puritan literature. The chapters that follow explore how several authors employ fe-male characters as part of their attempt, in Milton's words, to "justify the ways of God to men" (*PL* 1.26). I am particularly interested in the strategies by which these authors use Pauline theology to deflect onto women their ambivalence about such concepts as Original Sin, human depravity, and predestination. In identifying the theological origins of a sexism that offends twentieth-century readers, I hope to provide a method by which

45. John Bunyan, *The Life and Death of Mr. Badman* (London: Oxford University Press, 1929), pp. 110, 237, 229, 113, 119.
46. For a chilling example of how battered women feel that Scripture justifies their victimization, see Susan Brooks Thistlethwaite, "Every Two Minutes: Battered Women and Feminist Interpretation," in *Feminist Interpretation of the Bible*, pp. 96–107.

modern readers can appreciate the cultural and theological richness and complexity of these texts without feeling required to condone the sexist doctrines they espouse.

In her elaboration of a new feminist biblical hermeneutics, Fiorenza warns that "the pitfall to be avoided by feminist theology is apologetics, since an apologetics does not take the political implications of scriptural interpretation seriously." She argues that feminist theologians must work "to understand and interpret [scripture] in such a way that its oppressive and liberating power is clearly recognized . . . because the Bible still functions today as a religious justification and ideological legitimization of patriarchy."[47] Because Puritan literature participates in and attempts to derive its authority from the ideology of biblical patriarchy, a contextual reading of these works cannot evaluate them solely according to their *Sitz im Leben*, for no interpretive act is wholly detached and neutral. Any attempt at a purely "objective" evaluation of these texts ignores their power to speak across time and risks perpetuating their sexist assumptions. But because its authors place themselves self-consciously in the Pauline tradition, Puritan literature also offers the tools of prophetic critique with which to correct its own deformations. Like the feminist theologians who struggle to reclaim a Bible that, despite its patriarchal character, has shaped their identity and values in a positive way, I refuse to abandon Puritan literature.[48] But it is only by deploying "a hermeneutics of suspicion," by becoming what Judith Fetterley calls "a resisting reader,"[49] that one can hope to expose and neutralize the ideological assumptions that disfigure the literature of individual conscience and impassioned protest. In my discussion, therefore, I explore the representation of women in Puritan literature from the double perspective of a scholar

47. Fiorenza, *Bread Not Stone*, pp. 53, x, xi.
48. See Mary Ann Tolbert, "Defining the Problem: The Bible and Feminist Hermeneutics," *Semeia* 28 (1983): 113–26; and the essays by Letty M. Russell, Margaret A. Farley, Katherine Doob Sakenfeld, Rosemary Radford Ruether, and Elisabeth Schussler Fiorenza in *Feminist Interpretation of the Bible*.
49. See Judith Fetterley, *The Resisting Reader: A Feminist Approach to American Literature* (Bloomington: Indiana University Press, 1978).

versed in the Pauline origins of Puritan theology and a twentieth-century feminist skeptical of the Puritan argument for the subordination of women.

While I place these works clearly in the context of the seventeenth-century Puritan discussion of women, sexuality, and marriage, I am, like the Puritans, guilty of privileging the spirit, or at least the word, over the flesh: this book focuses not on the reality of Puritan domestic life but on how the Puritan theory of marriage and its spiritual significance influences the representation of women in literature.[50] Certainly some Puritan marriages were successful and satisfying and some not; perhaps some couples effected a respectful equality in their relationships. But in literary expression, an author's fantasies, fears, and theories about the world may develop unrestricted by reality. Puritan cases of conscience admit of circumstances in which a child may be justified in refusing to obey a parental command or in which a wife may be more intelligent and capable than her husband, but in art, such qualifications and exceptions need not arise.

I approach *The Faerie Queene* as a transitional Protestant text, aristocratic in its conception but Puritan in its leanings.[51] The juxtaposition of the Books of Holinesse and Chastitie allows an opportunity to consider the changes that occur in the representation of women, particularly in terms of their activity and independence, when the context becomes moral and domestic. As the hero of her book, Britomart shares the humanity of the other titular knights; she also shares their fallibility. A maiden warrior, restrained yet passionate, feminine yet aggressive, innocent yet sexual, she embodies the tension of potential toward both good and evil within the Judeo-Christian under-

50. Some influential studies of Puritan marriage and family life include William Haller and Malleville Haller, "The Puritan Art of Love," *Huntington Library Quarterly* 5 (1942): 235–72; Edmund Morgan, *The Puritan Family* (Boston: Trustees of the Public Library, 1944); Stone, *Family, Sex and Marriage*; and John Halkett, *Milton and the Idea of Matrimony: A Study of the Divorce Tracts and Paradise Lost* (New Haven: Yale University Press, 1970).

51. For a discussion of Spenser's position in relation to the militant Protestantism of the Leicester circle, see Anthea Hume, *Edmund Spenser: Protestant Poet* (Cambridge: Cambridge University Press, 1984).

standing of the human condition. Even though he uses Brit-omart as part of his program to teach his reader how to be a gentleman, Spenser carefully constructs her quest to prevent the reader from misinterpreting her passion as lustful or her independence as willful or normative. Her restoring the Amazon women "To mens subjection"[52] defines female virtue as the recognition of women's inferiority and a voluntary submission to male authority.

In *Paradise Lost,* the quality identified as "female" is Original Sin, which Milton has Michael call "effeminate slackness" (11.634). Milton separates this troublesome aspect of human nature from the man, figures it in the female, and then punishes her for it. In the allegory, each woman embodies the occasion for her lover's fall because she represents his particular weakness: Sin represents Satan's self-absorption, and Eve, Adam's sense of incompleteness. Their paradoxical condition embodies the central tension of *Paradise Lost,* that man can be "Sufficient to have stood, though free to fall" (*PL* 3.99). It remains to Christ to undo the sin of disobedience, expressing in himself the perfectly submissive female complement to God the Father.

Bunyan's location of sexuality, and therefore evil, in the womanly body requires that the displacement of the feminine become fully expressed structurally in *The Pilgrim's Progress.* Bunyan expresses Christiana's relationship to God as that of Bride to Bridegroom, but having established the Christian's metaphorical relationship to God within the normal sexual nexus, he transfers the metaphor to the male. Stand-fast, the male perfection of the idea of feminine virtue, usurps Christiana's role as heroine and as Bride; the type of "higher chastity," male chastity, Stand-fast becomes the exemplary Bride of Christ.

I close this book by examining two later responses to this Puritan literary phenomenon. In *Clarissa,* Samuel Richardson struggles to reconstitute the possibility of a heroic woman de-

---

52. Edmund Spenser, *The Faerie Queene,* in *Spenser: Poetical Works,* ed. J. C. Smith and E. de Selincourt (London: Oxford University Press, 1912), 5.7.42, hereafter cited in the text by book, canto, and stanza number.

spite the conflation of a woman's spiritual and physical condition prevalent in his culture. Clarissa's perfect obedience, her contempt for the flesh, and her holy death establish her purity, but only at the expense of her humanity: she becomes increasingly "other." Sanctified by her trials, Clarissa transcends her sex; Richardson's novel elevates one woman at the expense of womankind.

Hawthorne in *The Scarlet Letter* reconstructs the Puritan world in an attempt to expose its biases; he presents Hester's situation as a radical critique of Puritan sexual stereotyping. Hester escapes Clarissa's radical rejection of self because her pregnancy requires her to accept the material world. Hawthorne, however, cannot distance himself adequately from "the Puritan problem" because the transcendentalist's alienation of self from world, including the body, simply restates the Puritan problem with sexuality in other terms. The sin that intrigues Hawthorne in *The Scarlet Letter* is not the offstage sin of passion but the spiritual sin Chillingworth attempts to seduce Dimmesdale to commit. Dimmesdale becomes the "heroine" of *The Scarlet Letter*, structurally reenacting the artistic displacement of the feminine in Puritan allegory.

I

Spenser's Brides Errant

I

Edmund Spenser begins *The Faerie Queene* with a characteristically Protestant spiritual biography. Red Cross achieves his quest not through his own strength or special status but through faith troubled by a clear sense of personal insufficiency. Spenser, like later Puritan authors, creates an unidealized, fallible knight, who learns from experience to rely on faith alone; he expects his readers to apply that knight's experience to their own struggle toward faith. But within Red Cross's Protestant story is a female character who seems untroubled by the incipiently Puritan anxiety and self-doubt that plague Red Cross. Although Una is not the central figure in Book 1, she is important and active. It is she who initiates the quest, leaving her home in search of a champion for her people; it is her continuing fidelity and activity that enable Red Cross to complete his part of the quest.[1] In one sense, the love contest between Una and Duessa determines the plot of the book: the Legend of Holinesse closes with the slaying of the dragon, of course, but

1. A. C. Hamilton, *The Structure of Allegory in the Faerie Queene* (Oxford: Clarendon Press, 1961), p. 84.

also with the betrothal of the hero to the heroine and the rejection of Duessa's supposed claim.

The shift of subject from holiness in Book 1 to chastity in Book 3 reveals changes that occur in the representation of women, particularly in terms of their activity and independence, when the literary context shifts from the spiritual to the moral. Despite Una's importance to the plot of Book 1, Spenser pursues in the Legend of Holinesse a spiritual allegory that casts her as a part of Red Cross, rather than as a romance heroine in her own right. Britomart, the titular hero of Book 3, functions quite differently from Una, partly because she is the psychological focus of her story and partly because through her experience Spenser explores a virtue inextricably tied to human relationships and to the fact of sexuality. In turning from the Legends of Holinesse and Temperance to that of Chastitie, Spenser shifts his focus from the religious to the moral, from the male to the female, and consequently, from woman as embodied idea to woman as representative type, or Everywoman. Spenser's solutions to the problems he encounters in his allegorical treatment of Britomart because of this new focus on her representative womanhood anticipate the strategies later Puritan writers would use in their representation of female characters.

Spenser's central characters are dynamic figures, growing toward the perfection of their ideas.[2] But such minor characters as Una occupy more static allegorical roles, even when they are given psychological characterization. As William Oram points out, "She embodies [Red Cross's] truth or troth, his fidelity to the quest which he has begun." Because Spenser is more interested in what Una reveals about Red Cross's spiritual condition than in Una's own psychology, her position in the poem gravitates toward what Oram describes as "an allegorical counter," "shining with the light of its embodied idea."[3] Iconographically, Una transcends normal human experience by representing both Red Cross's faith and the True Church. Her wander-

2. See Van Dyke, *Fiction of Truth*, p. 252; William A. Oram, "Characterization and Spenser's Allegory," in *Spenser at Kalamazoo 1984* (Clarion: Clarion University of Pennsylvania, 1984), pp. 95–99.

3. Oram, "Characterization," pp. 111, 93.

ings, as John E. Hankins has shown, mirror those of the bride in the Song of Solomon and of the woman clothed with the sun in Revelations; her triumphal betrothal clearly identifies her with the Bride of the Lamb at the end of time.[4] Her importance as allegorical signifier overwhelms her individuality.

As the hero of her book, Britomart shares the humanity of the other titular knights; she also shares their fallibility. Most readers would agree with Mark Rose that "Britomart is not chastity personified; rather, as Spenser tells us, she is "the flowre of chastity" (III.xi.6)—that is, a chaste woman—just as Redcross is a holy man and certainly not, at the start of his story at any rate, holiness incarnate."[5] Because Britomart as a character is more like Red Cross and Guyon than like Una, one would expect that her quest would conform to the pattern established in Books 1 and 2, where the knights grow toward their virtues through trial and error, learning to resist temptation and to defend the principles they champion. Significantly, however, the heroine of Chastitie never experiences illicit desire or is subjected to any man's amorous advances; she never has to use her magic spear to protect her body from any real danger. Although she participates in the pattern of virtue-centered development that determines the representation of Spenser's central allegorical characters, Britomart is not allowed the range of growth and experience accorded Red Cross and Guyon.

Kathleen Williams, attempting to explain the shift from the single, unified stories of Books 1 and 2 to the parallel and only loosely connected plots of the third and fourth books, suggests that "to become truly and fully loving is not to be achieved by resisting a series of temptations and overcoming one final enemy; it is something to be worked out by trial and error."[6] The two processes she identifies, however, are not necessarily con-

---

4. See John E. Hankins, "Spenser and the Revelation of St. John," in *Essential Articles for the Study of Edmund Spenser*, ed. A. C. Hamilton (Hamden, Conn.: Archon, 1972), pp. 40–57.

5. Mark Rose, *Heroic Love: Studies in Sidney and Spenser* (Cambridge: Harvard University Press, 1968), p. 80.

6. Kathleen Williams, *Spenser's World of Glass: A Reading of "The Faerie Queene"* (Berkeley: University of California Press, 1966), p. 85.

tradictory: Red Cross and Guyon both work out their virtues through a series of temptations, some of which they successfully resist and others to which they respond "erroneously," as when Red Cross disarms by the fountain to dally with Duessa (1.7.2–7). Guyon can be sexually attracted to the bathing damzelles, and yet choose to refrain from acting on his impulse. But Spenser cannot allow Britomart to experience similar sexual temptation because she is a representative female character, an unmarried woman, whose chastity can be assured only by her continuously focused desire for Artegall.

While Spenser understands Britomart's chastity as both spiritual and physical, he places her virtue explicitly in the context of *female* chastity. It complements but cannot be precisely identified with Guyon's continence,[7] of which Belphoebe's chosen virginity seems to be the female counterpart. Britomart, because she has chosen her man, must remain single-mindedly devoted to him: were Britomart attracted to or even approached by any man except Artegall, she would be "unchaste." Thomas Overbury, in his popular poem *The Wife* (1613), expresses the prevalent Renaissance view of female responsibility for sexual misbehavior:

> in part to blame is she,
> Which hath *without consent* been only tride;
> He comes *too neere* that comes to be *denide*.[8]

7. See both Maureen Quilligan, *Milton's Spenser: The Politics of Reading* (Ithaca: Cornell University Press, 1983); and Frederick M. Padelford, "The Allegory of Chastity in *The Faerie Queene*," in *The Works of Edmund Spenser: A Variorum Edition*, ed. Padelford (Baltimore: Johns Hopkins University Press, 1934), for discussions of Books 2 and 3 as paired considerations of sexuality and continence. Quilligan suggests that the two books consider the "labyrinth of desire" from first a male and then a female perspective; Padelford argues that the Legend of Chastitie "logically" follows that of Temperance because chastity "is to all intents and purposes synonymous with continence when we think of that virtue in connection with women" (p. 323). Padelford also reveals the sexism latent in the understanding of chastity as a physical virtue: apparently unconscious of the double standard he expresses, Padelford explains that "chastity is not relative; either a woman is chaste or she is not" (p. 323).

8. Thomas Overbury, *The Wife*, in *The Miscellaneous Works in Prose and Verse of Sir Thomas Overbury, Knt.*, ed. Edward F. Rimbault (London: Reeves and Turner, 1890), lines 214–16.

As the story of Lucrece, so popular in Renaissance England, illustrates, even a rape would destroy a woman's claim to virtue unless she took violent action to repudiate her violated body. While Britomart's chastity cannot be conflated with physical integrity, Spenser seems to join his generation in placing it with virginity in the category of "once for all" virtues. The subsequent restrictions placed on Britomart's potential experiences require that Spenser abandon the simpler narrative technique of the earlier books in favor of one that allows his heroine to emerge unsullied, to gain knowledge, especially sexual knowledge, vicariously. Unlike Guyon, she brings into the world not impurity but an innocence that must be protected and preserved.[9] Spenser substitutes for her experience the adventures of other, conventionally feminine heroines, generating multiple plots that advance Britomart's story while limiting her activity.

Complementing Britomart's situation, the stories of Florimell and Amoret enact her experience of fear, confusion, and desire without exposing her to censure. Unlike the actively heroic Britomart, Florimell and Amoret conform to social expectations of femininity and female behavior. Spenser can allow Florimell and Amoret certain kinds of adventures which he must deny Britomart—being pursued by grisly fosters, attacked by ancient fishermen, tortured by Enchanters, and mauled by Lust. Florimell and Amoret do not incur as much censure for their attractiveness and its consequences as Britomart would, even though she is better equipped to defend herself. Their obvious helplessness and deference to male defense and assistance play into accepted ideals of womanhood so that, as long as they continue to shriek and run, no one will ask them what

9. See Milton, *Areopagitica* (W 4:311). Milton's comment on fugitive and cloistered virtues leads him naturally into praise of Guyon's well-exercised temperance. His belief that the exposure to temptation is a prerequisite to virtuous conduct does not seem to apply to Britomart, who is instinctively loyal to her first and only love. In his own poetic representation of female chastity in *Comus*, Milton, like Spenser, avoids having his heroine explicitly tempted. Her temptation, to taste of the monster's cup, is like Britomart's, displaced from the sexual realm to insure our right apprehension of her spiritual as well as physical integrity.

they were doing out alone. Britomart, on the other hand, has been actively seeking adventure.

The position of Florimell and Amoret as "allegorical counters" also contributes to their moral immunity. Confronted, they easily blend into Beauty pursued by Lust, or Love captured by Fear. Even so, Spenser makes sure that Amoret's vicious wound miraculously heals after Britomart rescues her:

> And every part to safety full sound,
> As she was never hurt, was soone restor'd:
> Tho when she felt her selfe to be unbound,
> And perfect hole, prostrate she fell unto the ground.
>
> [3.12.38]

Despite her spiritual chastity, Amoret must be restored to her physically intact condition before she can return to Scudamour.

Because he treats Britomart's pursuit of chastity in terms that directly reflect on everyday experience, Spenser has to allow carnal limitations to impinge on allegorical reality. The distinction between the male heroes and Britomart arises from the difficulty of treating a woman who represents Everywoman as a transcendently allegorical figure. The freedom allowed knights in allegorical romances to participate in fantastic events and to succumb, however briefly, to the allure of sexual sorcery does not extend to female characters when they are supposed to be models for female conduct. Thomas Roche, warning that Britomart's character is "thematic and allegorical" rather than "dramatic" or "novelistic," nevertheless concedes that "in Britomart, Spenser was able to make his allegorical method subsume the smaller, more human detail of psychological realism."[10] Responding to Roche, William Oram distinguishes "allegorical" from "novelistic" characterization, suggesting that characters in the novel are located in a specific social context with "a fixed past and an open future" but characters in allegory are "teleologically determined," possessing "a blank

10. Thomas P. Roche, Jr., *The Kindly Flame: A Study of the Third and Fourth Books of Spenser's "Faerie Queene"* (Princeton: Princeton University Press, 1964), pp. 51–52.

past and a fixed future."[11] But although Britomart's quest is certainly teleologically determined, she also has a fixed past that fixes her future, as does the web of consequences that circumscribe the seemingly open future of Oram's novelistic character. Britomart's particular social position as her father's only heir and as a woman determines both her future and the shape of her allegorical quest. Her quest is not so much virtue oriented as marriage oriented; she does not grow out of herself toward the embodiment of the ideal of chastity but grows up to be a model wife.

Unlike the other titular heroes, Britomart has not undertaken her quest at the behest of Gloriana. Although, as Van Dyke argues, "movement toward an unattainable referent is fundamental to *The Faerie Queene*,"[12] Britomart's referent is marriage to Artegall, and she achieves this goal in the course of the poem; the force that initiates her quest is not a royal command but divine providence revealing its will to her through the magic mirror. Oram argues that when Spenser gives a character such as Britomart a specific past, "the background serves primarily to define the character's future. It develops the meaning of her quest."[13] But only the female knight requires this explanatory history, because only in the case of a woman does independence and self-determination become problematic. The male protagonists, being both more broadly representative and more acceptably autonomous, do not require a doubly determined plot to explain or excuse their activity. In order to diffuse the social implications of Britomart's quest and to secure her ability to represent her virtue, Spenser must handle her more realistically, or "novelistically," than he does the male knights. Despite its allegorical nature, Britomart's story closely resembles what Nancy Miller calls the "euphoric" heroine's text, with its telos not of virtue but of marriage. Such an ending retrospectively redefines female independence by encoding it within the script of lawful heterosexual generation.[14]

11. Oram, "Characterization," pp. 96–98.
12. Van Dyke, *Fiction of Truth*, p. 282.
13. Oram, "Characterization," p. 97.
14. See Miller, *Heroine's Text*, p. xi. For a useful discussion of how the

Protestant companionate marriage—the telos of Britomart's quest—effectively channels and controls female power. Just as while extolling sexual passion within marriage, Spenser paints a grim picture of illicit passion and its consequences for women, so while arguing the Protestant case for mutuality within marriage, Spenser reinforces sexual hierarchy as natural and good. When Scudamour finds Amoret in the Temple of Venus, she sits "even in the lap of Womanhood" (4.10.52), surrounded by Womanhood's companions and attributes—Shamefastnesse, Cherefulnesse, Modestie, Curtesie, Silence, and Obedience. Spenser calls attention to the biblical source and Christian context of the last two virtues,

> Both linckt together never to dispart,
> Both gifts of God not gotten but from thence
> Both girlonds of his Saints against their foes offence.
> [4.10.51]

The stylized tableau recalls the picture of Charissa with her babes, which occupies the same canto in the Legend of Holinesse. Charissa's portrait stresses the chaste sexuality presented as a human ideal in Book 3. She is a woman "full of great love, but *Cupids* wanton snare / As hell she hated, chast in worke and will" (1.10.30); her suckling babes share their place about her with a pair of turtle doves, the emblem of loyalty in love. Together Womanhood and Charissa form a composite picture of the Christian wife—modest, loving, fruitful, and obedient. This "wife" is what Britomart must become.

Britomart's quest is about "right relations" or, specific to the treatment of her quest in the Legend of Chastitie, the part that loyalty, expressed as sexual fidelity, plays in effecting them. Her final task in Book 3 is not to champion chastity itself but to break down mental barriers between a newly married couple. In the 1596 expansion of *The Faerie Queene*, in order to realize

---

"romance plot" subsumes the "quest plot" in the nineteenth-century novel, see the opening chapter of DuPlessis, *Writing beyond the Ending.* I argue that the patterns identified in both Miller's and DuPlessis's books existed in Renaissance texts about women as well.

Britomart's victory over courtly love in the context of her own relationship with Artegall, Spenser defers the result of her defeat of the Enchanter Busirane. But in the 1590 edition, her courageous action allows her an immediate vision of "right relations," the subtleties of marital hierarchy and harmony.[15] In the last stanzas of the 1590 *Faerie Queene*, Spenser describes Amoret's initiation into true wifehood, using the image of the hermaphrodite, a common Renaissance figure for the union of man and woman in marriage.[16] The image expresses mutuality of desire, but the couple's behavior conforms to the conventional understanding of male and female sexual roles. Scudamour actively embraces Amoret, whose swoon is rendered in language resonant with overtones of sexual and spiritual ecstasy:

> But she faire Lady overcommen quight
> Of huge affection, did in pleasure melt,
> And in sweete ravishment pourd out her spright.
>   [3.12.45a]

Unlike the veiled hermaphrodite in the Temple of Venus, transcending literal sexuality as it transcends sexual difference, this image of male-female union remains on the human level. It derives from the Judeo-Christian conception of the married couple as "one flesh" (Gen. 2:24) and its attendant assumptions

15. C. S. Lewis first called attention to Spenser's concern that romantic love be brought under the auspices of Christian marriage, identifying *The Faerie Queene* as a revision of the courtly love tradition, in *The Allegory of Love: A Study in Medieval Tradition* (London: Oxford University Press, 1936). He points out, however, that for Spenser subordination within relationships was a fact of universal order, that a loving relationship does not necessarily require that the partners have equal authority or power within it. See his discussion of justice, p. 348. See also Christopher Hill, *Puritanism and Revolution: Studies in Interpretation of the English Revolution of the Seventeenth Century* (London: Secker and Warburg, 1958), pp. 367–94.

16. See A. Kent Hieatt, *Chaucer, Spenser, Milton: Mythopoeic Continuites and Transformations* (Montreal: McGill-Queen's University Press, 1975), p. 82. For a full discussion of possible literary and iconographic sources for the hermaphrodite figure, as well as its role in providing closure to the 1590 *Faerie Queene*, see Donald Cheney, "Spenser's Hermaphrodite and the 1590 *Faerie Queene*," *PMLA* 87 (1972): 192–200.

of female subordination: "But I would have you know, that the head of every man is Christ; and the head of the woman is the man; and the head of Christ is God. . . . For the man is not of the woman; but the woman of the man. Neither was the man created for the woman; but the woman for the man" (1 Cor. 11:3, 8–9). Britomart, "half envying their blesse" (3.12.46a), receives a vision of her own "like happinesse" within a Christian marriage, in which heterosexual friendship and mutual respect do not preclude hierarchical relation. It is precisely in the context of Christian companionate marriage that the restrictions on female independence have to be "lovingly" insisted upon. In the light of the equality of all believers, the "naturalness" of social and sexual roles are no longer so obvious.

II

Uneasy about female sexual desire, Spenser carefully constructs Britomart's quest to prevent his reader from misinterpreting her passion as lustful or her independence as willful or normative. Britomart awakens to sexual desire in the fallen world, with all its murky ambiguities and complex motivations. By adapting the courtly love trope of "the ulcer of love" to Britomart's specific situation, Spenser reveals the problematic nature of female erotic desire. She describes her incipient sexual awareness in terms of her menses:

> Sithens it hath infixed faster hold
> Within my bleeding bowels, and so sore
> Now ranckleth in this same fraile fleshly mould,
> That all mine entrailes flow with poysnous gore.
> [3.2.39]

As Van Dyke points out, "Britomart's love is a profoundly ambivalent, even amoral force."[17] Although her emotion has been divinely incited and sanctioned, it can only be described in

17. Van Dyke, *Fiction of Truth*, p. 267.

the language of illicit passion drawn from the conventions of Renaissance sonnet sequences, and it is compared to the destructive passion of female characters in Ovid's *Metamorphoses*. Glauce initially fears that her charge has succumbed to some "filthy lust, contrarie unto kind" (3.2.40), like that of the Ovidian perverts Myrrha, Biblis, and Pasiphae. Glauce's function, Oram believes, is precisely to help Britomart "distinguish her feelings from those of other, disaster-prone, literary models."[18] Yet both Britomart and Glauce respond to her passion as a potentially disastrous threat to her life and her community.

Even Britomart's name illustrates this danger. Thomas Roche, drawing on an earlier article by Merritt Hughes, offers as a source for Britomart's name and characterization the young women in the Virgilian poem *Ciris*: Scylla, who passionately loves her father's enemy, and Britomartis, who fled into the sea to escape the same man's passion. Roche comments that, in conflating these two women, Spenser dissociates chastity from virginity and links it to passionate love and appropriate surrender in marriage.[19] But both the Virgilian analogues and the more readily apparent significance of Britomart's name—martial Britonesse[20]—reveal more than passionate love channeled and sanctioned through marriage. The origins and meanings of Britomart's name embody the paradoxical nature of her sexuality and independence. She is the maiden warrior, restrained yet passionate, feminine yet aggressive, innocent yet sexual. Ungoverned, her sexual passion would threaten, like Scylla's, both herself and the political order dependent on her cooperation.

Only chaste love, which channels female sexuality into lawful generation, provides a safe outlet for female sexual passion. The description of Womanhood in the Temple of Venus, the model for the kind of wifehood Britomart will attain, stresses that such continence begins in eyesight:

---

18. Oram, "Characterization," p. 117.
19. Roche, *Kindly Flame*, pp. 53–54.
20. See Joel Jay Belson, "The Names in *The Faerie Queene*" (Ph.D. diss., Columbia University, 1964), pp. 94–99.

> Her name was *Womanhood*, that she exprest
> By her sad semblant and demeanure wyse:
> For stedfast still her eyes did fixed rest,
> Ne rov'd at random after gazers guyse,
> Whose luring baytes oftimes doe heedlesse harts entyse.
>
> [4.10.49]

This passage emphasizes the extreme modesty and reserve necessary to insure female sexual purity. Malecasta reveals her lustfulness through her ungoverned eyes:

> Her wanton eyes, ill signes of womanhed,
> Did roll too lightly, and too often glaunce,
> Without regard of grace, or comely amenaunce.
>
> [3.1.41]

The ill-matched Helenore begins her escapade by returning Paridell's leer with "one firie dart, whose hed / Empoisned was with privy lust, and gealous dred" (3.9.28). As her plight suggests, the line between chastity and catastrophe is a very fine one: concupiscence of the eyes opens an irreparable breach in the ramparts.[21] In giving way to her animal impulses, actuated by eyesight, Hellenore becomes, in effect, a beast; she also destroys the world in which she lives, firing her husband's house to achieve her desire. Like the virtues that bar Destruction's strength at the close of Shelley's *Prometheus Unbound*, Britomart's chastity imposes precarious order on the chaos of sexual potential within her.[22]

As soon as Spenser reveals that Britomart is in love, he demonstrates both the cause of her passion and its justification: she falls in love by means of a magic globe that

---

21. See Nathaniel Hawthorne, *The Scarlet Letter*, in *The Works of Nathaniel Hawthorne*, Centenary Edition, ed. Fredson Bowers, 16 vols. (Columbus: Ohio State University Press, 1962), 1:200–1; also the speech in Milton's *Comus* beginning "But when lust . . ." (lines 463–75).

22. See *Prometheus Unbound* (act 4, lines 562–64): "Gentleness, Virtue, Wisdom, and Endurance, / These are the seals of that most firm assurance / Which bars the pit over Destruction's strength." *Shelley's Poetry and Prose*, ed. Donald Reiman and Sharon B. Powers (New York: Norton, 1977).

> vertue had, to shew in perfect sight,
> What ever thing was in the world contaynd,
> Betwixt the lowest earth and heavens hight,
> So that it to the looker appertaynd.
>
> [3.2.19]

Her marriage is arranged not by her earthly father but by divine providence. Despite this assurance that the revealed knight will be the proper one for Britomart to fix her affections upon, the narrative voice insists that, when she faced the glass and wondered "Whom fortune for her husband would allot" (3.2.23), her curiosity evinced no lust, "For she was pure from blame of sinfull blot / Yet wist her life at last must lincke in that same knot" (3.2.23). Britomart recognizes in the vision of her future lover only her social responsibility to marry.[23] She turns away ignorant of her incipient emotional attachment, her mind as "chaste" as her body is virginal.

That her passions and desires do not precede the presence of their proper object reinforces the idea of her purity. Instead of learning about love and "right relations" through trial and error, she practices chastity instinctively. The love that possesses her is an alien passion, so foreign to her that she fears it is unnatural, confiding to her nurse,

> Nor man it is, nor other living wight;
> For then some hope I might unto me draw,
> But th' only shade and semblant of a knight,
> Whose shape or person yet I never saw.
>
> [3.2.38]

Although Britomart becomes convinced, through Glauce's counsel, that her love is not "lewdly bent" (3.2.43), she still distrusts the legitimacy of her passion. This energy, which could be either concupiscence or virtuous love at first sight, can

---

23. Kathleen Williams also makes this point in *Spenser's World of Glass*, pp. 95–96, but I find her discussion marred by a lack of sensitivity to the sexism of her own language and assumptions. Williams considers Britomart's weakness to be her "feminine side" (p. 112), her "pity and fellow feeling" (p. 111), and Artegall's failing is his "effeminate submissiveness" (p. 168).

only be defined by appeal to a higher authority. Merlin must authorize her passion before she will assent to its power.

In order to justify Britomart's feelings, Merlin rejects the idea that her attachment is willful or involves free choice:

> It was not, Britomart, thy wandring eye,
> Glauncing unwares in charmed looking glas,
> But the streight course of heavenly destiny,
> Led with eternall providence, that has
> Guided thy glaunce, to bring his will to pas.
>
> [3.3.24]

He reassures her that her apparently "wandring eye" is really under divine control. Her love becomes not so much a personal passion as a public duty and a moral choice. Merlin, standing in for her father and for patriarchy embodied in the divine order, admonishes her, "Therefore submit thy wayes unto his will, / And do by all dew meanes thy destiny fulfill" (3.3.24). Because she is a pure and obedient girl, her personal inclination perfectly harmonizes with her public and filial duty. Like Christiana in *The Pilgrim's Progress*, she moves toward completion in marriage; her quest becomes an exercise in obedience, not in independence.[24]

The events framing Britomart's quest authorize her activity and safeguard her innocence. Unlike Una, who is always a "bride," awaiting the promised return of her beloved, which can only come about "in the fullness of time," Britomart will become a wife in this world, the world of human experience and the world of the poem. Her story has a predicted and predictable close, which both proleptically and retrospectively shapes her quest: "Long time ye both in armes shall beare great sway, / Till thy wombes burden thee from them do call" (3.3.28). Britomart's marriage to Artegall, as it confirms the prophecies, retrospectively defines her quest and interprets her behavior. Her activity and independence receive approval in the context

24. For discussions of similar patterns in eighteenth- and nineteenth-century fiction, see DuPlessis, *Writing beyond the Ending*, chap. 1, on the suppression of the quest plot in the marriage plot; and Miller, *Heroine's Text*, chap. 1, on the integration of the female hero into the social order through marriage.

of her sacred virginity, sacred because pledged to a particular man. The wounds she receives at the hands of Gardante and the Enchanter Busirane, because they represent her weakness for Artegall and not desire for another man, become morally neutral. When Artegall disarms her of her magic spear, her chastity is not called into question because it is Artegall who overwhelms her. Spenser has carefully built into his narrative evidence that will elicit from his readers the "appropriate" response to Britomart's passion—her love is, after all, preordained.

The moral ambiguity of female sexuality, which is latent in Britomart's character, becomes obvious a century later in Richardson's less artfully constructed *Pamela*. Through his manipulation of narrative events, Richardson attempts to neutralize the moral significance of Pamela's sexual awareness. Her attraction to Squire B—— does not indicate her lack of virtue because he becomes her husband: her marriage retrospectively sanctions her passions. For this reason, Pamela is expected to be excused for returning to his custody at the one point when she seems safely out of his clutches. If Squire B—— had then raped her, she would have been "asking for it," but since she judged rightly that he meant to do honorably by her, she is "innocent." Conversely, Richardson's Clarissa is aware that her past actions would be reinterpreted should she marry Lovelace; her refusal demonstrates to the world that the rape was a rape and not a seduction. So, too, Britomart, in marrying Artegall, fixes the interpretation of her attraction to him as a chaste emotion.

III

But Spenser cannot rest with the *correctio* of Britomart's marriage. When the as-yet-unidentified Britomart unseats Guyon, the narrator offers him this consolation: "For not thy fault, but secret powre unseene, / That spear enchaunted was, which layd thee on the greene." (3.1.7). While Britomart's spear and armor figure forth her chaste condition, they also represent her special prerogative as royalty; like Arthur's diamond shield

and Red Cross's inherited armor of Christ, Britomart's accesso-
ries indicate her political role and unique social position. As a
representative of Queen Elizabeth, she achieves personal power
inaccessible to other women. Britomart's successes in com-
bat—her rescuing the one knight against six, her overcoming
Marinell, her victory at the Tournament of the Girdle (4.4)—all
depend on the magic power of her spear. Without it, Britomart
would not be able to defend herself against the abilities of such a
knight as Guyon. Indeed, she would not be able to be a knight at
all. Deprived of this magic spear, Britomart reverts to a "feminine role"; in her nearly fatal hand-to-hand encounter with
Artegall, the only thing that saves her is the effect of her virginal beauty on Artegall's wonder and pity. Her quest stands not
as a validation of female autonomy and self-determination in
general but as a model for queenly behavior.

Britomart's role as an aspect of the chastity of Queen Elizabeth also complicates Spenser's handling of her sexuality. As
in Milton's *Comus*, where the chastity of the Lady, performed
by a titled young woman, is tested in terms of thirst rather than
of sexuality, decorum requires that Spenser protect his heroine
from any compromising situation: one simply does not represent a capricious monarch from whom one desires patronage as
anything but unimpeachable. Yet Britomart shares Elizabeth's
peculiar position as female suitor. Both women must take an
active role in the initiation of their courtships, Britomart because she, not Artegall, has received the vision of her future
match, Elizabeth because she has no father to act for her and no
subject dare presume so much. Spenser's problem, then, is to
offer an acceptable delineation of female courtship.

But desire usually initiates courtship, and to accord such
motivation is to attribute sexuality to the suitor, a condition
unacknowledged by Queen Elizabeth. In her speeches, Elizabeth referred to herself as king and prince, not simply as
queen; to address her troops, she wore armor and young men's
military clothing.[25] Lisa Jardine argues that in both her political

---

25. See, for example, Elizabeth's speech to the troops at Tilbury and speech
before her last Parliament in *The Female Spectator*, ed. Mary R. Mahl and
Helene Koon (Old Westbury, N.Y.: Feminist Press, 1977), pp. 48–51.

role and her iconographic presence, Elizabeth "stood in" for the absent male authority of the Tudor family: "On all public occasions Elizabeth I herself was metamorphosed into a female personification, an emblem (who could acceptably be of the female sex without any sense of inferiority) . . . , which removed from Elizabeth the taint of her sex, and endowed her instead with abstract and generalised authority."[26] With Una, Spenser achieves in the literary context what Elizabeth's court effected in the political realm: her emblematic virginity neutralizes her sexual presence. But in discussing the Protestant ideal of chastity within marriage through Britomart, Spenser cannot side-step the fact of her sexuality. In order to avoid presenting his sovereign as sexually interested, Spenser divides her image into "mirrours more than one" (3.proem.5)—Gloriana and Belphoebe embodying the perfection of her "rule" and "rare chastitee" in her public persona, Britomart and Amoret representing the desideratum of chaste marital love potentially available in her private life.

Britomart's role as Arthur's chastity[27] at once distorts her role as a chaste woman and diminishes the danger of the trials she encounters. She does not pursue Florimell, as do the rest of the knights, intent on "beauties chace," but why should she, a woman, be praised for being unmoved by the beauty of another woman?[28] Despite her incandescent beauty, Florimell does not represent a potential rival to Artegall in Britomart's affections. Similarly, Malecasta's mistaking Britomart for a male knight turns a potential instance of constancy and virtue into an amusing farce: Britomart does not realize that Malecasta's attentions constitute flirtation, and although she reacts violently on discovering someone in her bed, Malecasta does not pose any serious danger to her physical or spiritual purity. Spenser uses Britomart's ambiguous allegorical gender to elide questions about the real-life appropriateness of female sexual independence.

26. Lisa Jardine, *Still Harping on Daughters: Women and Drama in the Age of Shakespeare* (Totowa, N.J.: Barnes and Noble, 1983), p. 173.

27. See Spenser to Raleigh, in *Poetical Works*, p. 407.

28. Cheney, "Spenser's Hermaphrodite," notes that Britomart's indifference, rather than active chastity, governs her behavior in this scene.

Artegall's fall into the power of the Amazon Radigund and Britomart's response to his predicament provide a final correction to any erring tendency to read Britomart's quest as an affirmation of independence and power for all women. Unlike Britomart and her prototype Elizabeth, Radigund and her women have subverted the "natural" order in their willful disruption of male hierarchy. Radigund challenges men to battle and, when she wins, humiliates them by treating them like women:

> First she doth them of warlike armes despoile,
> And cloth in womens weedes: And then with threat
> Doth them compell to worke, to earne their meat,
> To spin, to card, to sew, to wash, to wring.
>
> [5.4.31]

Artegall, the knight of justice, shocked by the injustice of this activity, sends a challenge and foolishly accepts Radigund's conditions:

> That if I vanquishe him, he shall obay
> My law, and ever to my lore be bound,
> And so will I, if me he vanquish may.
>
> [5.4.49]

Although he overpowers her, he can't kill her. He responds to her female beauty and helplessness as he responded to Britomart's in their martial encounter: "At sight thereof his cruell minded hart / Empierced was with pittifull regard" (5.5.13). Artegall's refusal to kill Radigund because of pity induced by her female beauty and helplessness redefines his inability to fight the unhelmeted Britomart. His astonished adoration, which seemed so laudable when he was confronted with Britomart's chaste beauty and virtue, becomes evidence of his folly in the face of the bloodthirsty, lustful Amazon. It figures forth his uxoriousness—not his right admiration of a virtuous woman but his tendency to overvalue female beauty in general.[29] His

29. Mark Rose comments that "in ceasing to be a woman hater, Artegall has gone to the other extreme and become an idolator, turning his wonder into religion" (*Heroic Love*, p. 105), and identifies his idolatry as his tendency to

earlier worshipful response—"At last fell humbly downe upon his knee, / And of his wonder made religion" (4.6.22)—requires reevaluation.

Radigund's excessive aggression in war and love qualify the reader's understanding of Britomart's knightly activity as a special case. If, as A. C. Hamilton suggests, "Radigund expresses Britomart's womanly pride to which Artegall submits,"[30] then the message of Artegall's experience in Radigund's hands is that, in yielding power to Britomart through his love for her, Artegall has upset the "natural" hierarchy and unleashed chaos. Since Radigund is Britomart's rival, she also represents Elizabeth's archenemy, Mary Queen of Scots. Her unnatural aggression, instanced in her desire to degrade her captives, underscores the dignity of Britomart/Elizabeth's exercise of power and proves her authority to be unique and providential. Spenser disassociates the disruptive potential of female autonomy from the heroine, simultaneously praising her exceptional abilities and privilege and demonstrating how common women would abuse that privilege.

Radigund recognizes Artegall's superiority, however much she would rather not admit it. To compensate for her political helplessness, she resorts to exploiting the political power, or "maisterie," which Artegall, out of courtesy, has yielded to her.[31] Like Britomart, Radigund cannot win a battle in her own right, but unlike Britomart, who listens to Glauce's counsel and curbs her wrath in her battle with Arthur, Radigund determines to prevail. She relies on treachery, the exploitation of chivalric attitudes toward women, to gain her ends. Artegall yields to her "of his own accord" (5.5.17) because he pities her. Radigund herself later admits that "not my valour, but his owne brave mind" has subjected him to her "unequall might" (5.5.32), but she does not refrain from exploiting that power.

---

effeminacy (p. 107). Williams also refers to Artegall's pity as "effeminate submissiveness" (*Spenser's World of Glass*, p. 168). See my chapter on *Paradise Lost*, where I argue that effeminacy, or "effeminate slackness," becomes the metaphor for original sin in Milton's poem.

30. Hamilton, *Structure of Allegory*, p. 185.
31. See Williams, *Spenser's World of Glass*, p. 171.

Radigund's uncontrolled violence, or unfeminine aggression, transforms into nearly uncontrollable lust upon Artegall's surrender. Having given herself "licentious libertie," Radigund becomes the sexual aggressor. Although he does not offer evidence of literal promiscuity, Spenser emphasizes the incontinence of her desire, for "her wandring fancie after lust did raunge" (5.5.26) and her perception of the politics of her situation can barely channel her passion:

> Yet would she not thereto yeeld free accord,
> To serve the lowly vassall of her might,
> And of her servant make her soveraryne Lord,
> So great her pride, that she such basenesse much abhord.
>
> [5.5.27]

While she wishes to transform her control over Artegall from physical constraint to emotional and sexual attachment, Radigund quite explicitly wants to remain the dominant member in the relationship. She would rule at home as well as abroad. Britomart exhibits this same tendency toward "willfulness" (cf. 4.6.42–46), but her unusual self-restraint and sense of civic responsibility have successfully governed her passion.[32]

Like Adam in *Paradise Lost*, Artegall overvalues the female, disrupting natural hierarchy, the right exercise of marital relations under the auspices of justice; like Eve, Britomart must restore marital order by rescuing her man from his persecutor (in Adam's case, despair) and then voluntarily submitting to and reinstituting the "proper" patriarchal order. Her behavior

---

32. T. K. Dunseath, *Spenser's Allegory of Justice in Book Five of the Faerie Queene* (Princeton: Princeton University Press, 1968), assumes that Britomart's "jealous fears were unfounded" (p. 178). Despite Artegall's capitulation in battle and his subsequent submission, courtesy, and pleasantries, we are to believe that "Yet never meant he in his noble mind, / To his owne absent love to be untrew" (5.5.56). Artegall, as a sexually besieged Penelope figure, must wait patiently until Britomart, as Ulysses, comes to rescue him. This inversion of the Ulysses-Penelope situation will then be set aright by Britomart, who will voluntarily become Penelope, the patient wife who waits at home, at the end of Book 5, Canto 7. Dunseath argues that the suppression of her jealousy and her desire to keep Artegall at home (5.6.44) indicate Britomart's "maturity" and education into perfect wifehood (pp. 179–80). Clearly, this self-effacement represents her attempt to repress any Radigund-like tendency to dominance.

on this occasion must in some way revise our understanding of the events preceding it. A. C. Hamilton suggests that "when [Britomart] dresses [Artegall] in his armour, she restores the manhood which she had taken from him. Now they have achieved the true marriage state, in which each yields the 'maisterie' to the other."[33] But while Britomart does in fact restore Artegall's manhood by this action, she also surrenders the "maisterie" he had incorrectly yielded to her. Britomart's deep aversion to "that lothly uncouth sight, / Of men disguiz'd in womanishe attire" (5.7.37), requires the reader to reconsider the appropriateness of her own cross-dressing. She has assumed a male identity as a protective disguise, in much the same way as Viola will do in *Twelfth Night* or Rosalind in *As You Like It*. It is a matter of expediency, not revolution. In an instance of poetic justice, Britomart, who seemingly subverted "nature" in taking up arms, uses her political power to reinforce patriarchal order. It is she who

> The liberty of women did repeale,
> Which they had long usurpt; and them restoring
> To mens subjection, did true Justice deale.
> (5.7.42)

By having Britomart, the most aggressive, active good woman in the poem, articulate this doctrine of female subordination, Spenser anticipates Shakespeare, who places the speech on appropriate female submissiveness in the mouth of Kate at the end of *The Taming of the Shrew*. Her conversion lends the statement a peculiar kind of authority.

IV

At the beginning of Britomart's quest, the narrator attributes the decline of women warriors to male jealousy and points to a similar pattern of conservatism in the politics of his own time:

33. Hamilton, *Structure of Allegory*, p. 185.

> envious Men fearing their rules decay,
> Gan coyne streight lawes to curb their liberty;
> Yet sith they warlike armes have layd away,
> They have exceld in artes and pollicy,
> That now we foolish men that prayse gin eke t'envy.
>
> [3.2.2]

But while Spenser recognizes abuses of patriarchal order and credits individual women with intelligence and ability, he has too much invested in the status quo to make any commitment to change. He praises the exceptions as exceptions,[34] but offers as the inevitable outcome of women's sexual and political activity Radigund and her society turned upside down:

> Such is the crueltie of womankynd,
> When they have shaken off the shamefast band,
> With which wise Nature did them strongly bynd,
> T'obay the heasts of mans well ruling hand,
> That then all rule and reason they withstand,
> To purchase a licentious libertie.
> But vertuous women wisely understand,
> That they were borne to base humilitie,
> Unlesse the heavens them lift to lawfull soveraintie.
>
> [5.5.25]

The equation of political autonomy with sexual misconduct is inescapable. Not only among the Amazons but in Britain and Faery Land, women who achieve independence of men descend into "licentious libertie." Anticipating Bunyan's reasoning in *A Case of Conscience Resolved*, the poem argues that the proof of a woman's wisdom and of her sexual virtue rests in her voluntary submission to male authority.

In the Legend of Holinesse, Una's symbolic role so neutralizes her sexual presence that when Una orders Duessa stripped, Duessa's sexual humiliation and the knights' horrified revulsion in no way reflect on Una herself. Although the narrator calls Duessa's genitals "the shame of all her kind" (1.8.48), Una

---

34. See Jardine, *Still Harping on Daughters*, chap. 2, for a provocative but controversial discussion of the limits of female achievement in academics and politics during the Renaissance.

is neither shamed nor implicated. Duessa's monstrous sexuality—all sexuality—has nothing to do with her. But in the Legend of Chastitie, because each female character represents an aspect of Britomart's struggle toward chaste sexuality, the innocence of any female desire, even Britomart's, is called into question by their licentiousness. When Malecasta pants with incontinent desire, when Hellenore frolics among the satyrs, when Radigund lusts after the defeated Artegall, Spenser indirectly explores Britomart's control of her own sexuality. Britomart's restrained passion and their abandoned desire are of the same kind. As the Virgilian origin of her name and Glauce's frantic response to her lovesickness indicate, Britomart's sexuality contains this potential destructiveness. Although, as I have argued, Spenser attempts to fix our understanding of Britomart as a chaste, good woman, her chastity is never secure; sexual desire is the danger within her that she must continually practice to control and subdue. Like the wombs of Spenser's female monsters, Britomart's "entrailes flow with poysonous gore" (3.2.39). The connection between female sexual licentiousness and Britomart's own sexuality looks forward to the Puritan location of sin within all female bodies and the consequent insistence on female subordination within marriage.

2

Effeminate Slackness Substantially Expressed: Woman as Scapegoat in *Paradise Lost*

I

In the second book of *Paradise Lost,* Milton describes an encounter between Satan and Sin, Satan's daughter, lover, and other self, which explores the nature of sinfulness and the individual's relation to it while parodying conservative rhetoric about domestic relations. The preternatural guilty sympathy between Satan and Sin represents a perversion of the healthy mutuality expressed in Adam and Eve's prelapsarian relationship, while the exaggerated formality of their marital roles foreshadows the depths of hypocrisy to which Adam and Eve will descend after the Fall. The passage prepares the reader to question the imperfect, because fallen, logic of Adam's and Eve's mutual recriminations and prefigures the stages of their reconciliation.

But the relationship between Satan and Sin illuminates that of Adam and Eve even more fully. Like Sin, Eve derives her existence from some need in her husband, who becomes in some sense her "father." Each woman embodies the occasion of her lover's fall because she represents his particular weakness—Sin, Satan's self-absorption, and Eve, Adam's sense of incompleteness. These weaknesses are mirror faults: each male sins against God by loving a creature more than he loves his God, although their loves have opposite impulses, one toward self-love and one toward self-denial. The women, therefore, represent opposing weaknesses, filling the vacuum that their husbands' personalities create. Sin is passive and dependent; Eve, active and independent. Their presence does not precipitate but allows the dramatization of their husbands' falls. As manifestations of their husbands' "effeminate slackness" (11.634), Sin and Eve, with their fellow victim, the unfortunate serpent, are at once dependent and responsible. The paradoxical nature of their condition embodies a central tension in *Paradise Lost*, that man can be "Sufficient to have stood, though free to fall" (3.99).

The question of Eve's sufficiency and the responsibility it entails has occasioned a great deal of critical debate in this century, particularly in relation to Eve's subordinate status. Despite the careful, cogent scholarship of Stella Revard and Diane McColley, modern, particularly feminist, readers continue to be troubled by Milton's presentation of Eve as inferior yet complete, subordinate yet sufficient. Sandra Gilbert traces the influence of what she terms Milton's "paradigmatic patriarchal poetry" on women writers in the nineteenth and early twentieth centuries. She concludes that "the story that Milton, 'the first of the masculinists,' most notably tells to women is of course the story of woman's secondness, her otherness, and how that otherness leads inexorably to her demonic anger, her sin, her fall, and her exclusion from that garden of the gods which is also, for her, the garden of poetry."[1] In labeling Milton "the first of the masculinists" and attributing "demonic anger" to Eve, Gilbert betrays both her polemical tendency and her willingness to perpetuate the tradition of "misreading" that she attributes to women readers of *Paradise Lost*.

Joan Webber attempts to correct this "misreading." She

1. Sandra Gilbert, "Patriarchal Poetry and Women Readers: Reflections on Milton's Bogey," *PMLA* 93 (1978): 370. See Diane Kelsey McColley's work, particularly *Milton's Eve* (Urbana: University of Illinois Press, 1983); and Stella P. Revard, "Eve and the Doctrine of Responsibility in *Paradise Lost*," *PMLA* 88 (1973): 69–78.

places the poem in "the historical and literary contexts which may not justify Milton, but do explain him," sensibly pointing out that Milton "himself was among the first who saw and helped to define the problems of our age," including the contradiction between external authority and individual freedom, between hierarchy and equality in the spirit.[2] She cautions that "we attack Milton with weapons he himself gave us the power to create." But in emphasizing the revolutionary aspects of Milton's treatment of women in the poem, Webber dismisses the real discomfort female readers feel when they read *Paradise Lost*. Because Milton wrote on the threshold of the modern age, because "when he did raise issues involving women's importance and women's rights, he was awkwardly and imperfectly breaking ground,"[3] *Paradise Lost* embodies his struggles, his ambivalence, and his uncertainty: it sends a double message.

Christine Froula proposes a kind of feminist reading that would not, as Joan Webber fears, "let the literature of our common humanity be needlessly sacrificed."[4] Defining a feminist reader as one who "raises questions about the sources, motives, and interests of [literary] authority," Froula uses Milton's portrayal of Eve's awakening and education to her own secondariness as a proof text for the relationship "canonical authority institutes between itself and its believers in converting them from the authority of their own experience to a 'higher' authority." She posits as reader an external "Eve," a woman who speaks from the authority of her own experience, "from her body, from an experience that exists outside of patriarchal authority." This woman's reading, Froula argues, would demystify the poem so that it might become "a cultural artifact situated in history, its power analyzable as that of an ancient and deeply ingrained pattern in Western thought, reinvented to serve the interests of modern society and realized in language of unsurpassed subtlety and *explicable* sublimity." In fact, however Froula's discussion of *Paradise Lost* fails to achieve this goal.

2. Joan Webber, "The Politics of Poetry: Feminism and *Paradise Lost*," in *Milton Studies*, vol. 14, ed. James D. Simmonds (Pittsburgh: University of Pittsburgh Press, 1980), p. 4.

3. Ibid., p. 6.

4. Ibid., p. 5.

She discusses the poem not as a valuable cultural artifact but as an illustration of how totalitarian authority crushes opposition: *Paradise Lost* becomes "a violent parable of *gnosis* punished."[5]

Froula reads *Paradise Lost* out of its literary and historical context—comparing Eve's silencing to the fate of first-century Christian gnosticism—because to read the poem in its context complicates the parable. In context, the poem becomes neither a "bogey" nor an "artifact" but a troubling piece of literature. Froula need not resort to gnosticism to find a precursor for her ideal reader's sense of personal authority. Milton himself would do. Froula's feminist reader, who speaks from the authority of her own experience, is a secular version of the Christian dissenter. Her authority derives from within herself but not from her "body." To define a woman's perspective as purely biological, a mistake Froula scrupulously avoids in her opening discussion, perpetuates the patriarchal attitude toward women as tokens, ciphers, and objects. The feminist reader speaks, like all dissenters, not from body but from conscience, from a moral perception of the world. As the work of modern Christian feminist theologians demonstrates, such dissent is the logical development of the Gospel of human redemption Milton espoused. But troubling aspects of *Paradise Lost* must neither be dismissed as anachronistic nor explained without reference to its historical context, because the tensions female readers identify within Milton's poem are the contradictions that inform his religious tradition and remain at the center of theological and social debate today. I propose to read *Paradise Lost* as a scholar and a feminist, from within and without, to try to reconcile the attention to religious and historical context Joan Webber commends with sensitivity to the inconsistency in Milton's message concerning women's moral sufficiency that feminist readings recognize.

II

Toward the close of their debate about separating to tend the garden, Adam warns Eve that, although God created man per-

---

5. Christine Froula, "When Eve Reads Milton: Undoing the Canonical Economy," *Critical Inquiry* 10 (1983): 322, 328–29, 335, 335–36, 329.

fect, "within himself / The danger lies, yet lies within his power" (9.348–49). This understanding of human nature, even prelapsarian human nature, as profoundly paradoxical derives from Paul; from Paul, Milton receives the metaphor that provides a literary solution. In his analogy that male corresponds to female as spirit to flesh, Paul provides a "logic" by which Milton can artistically represent the paradoxical disobedience of a sinless, perfect, new man. While Adam's temptation comes from "within," Eve, "his other self," is the immediate cause of his disobedience. Separated from the self and reincarnated as the woman, a man's impulse toward personal comfort and the things of this world can be subordinated and controlled. As Michael curiously explains to Adam during his vision of human history, man's woe does not proceed from woman—from the actual physical person—but from "man's effeminate slackness"—from the aspect of human nature that woman embodies. Sin results from a man's inability to keep his "feminine" weaknesses, his "female" half, in check.

Readers who do not respond with horror to the predicament of the character Sin insist on reading her as pure personification; as personification, she is certainly vivid. She springs fullgrown from Satan's brain, her birth simultaneous with his willful decision to exalt himself as his "god" above God. Whereas Adam's recognition of his own need for fellowship apparently initiates the creation of Eve, Satan's refusal to recognize his secondary, contingent nature begets Sin. She herself identifies the time of her birth as during the assembly of conspirators in heaven, the council at which Satan declares that he acknowledges "none before us, self-begot, self-rais'd / By our own quick'ning power" (5.860–61). Sin is a material projection of Satan's sinfulness; their subsequent incestuous intercourse, played out spatially in the allegory but actually coincident with the sinful thought, enacts Satan's self-love; as Sin reminds him, "Thy self in me thy perfect image viewing / Becam'st enamour'd" (2.764–65). Their union is narcissistic as well as incestuous. Satan's cautious recognition of her at the gates of Hell illustrates his growing self-awareness, for if Satan is to recognize Sin, now horribly deformed, he must first recognize his own fallen self.

But while Sin clearly functions as an allegorical figure, embodying "sinfulness" and dramatizing in her present physical relationship with Satan an individual's intimacy with sin, she is also a woman, who has been given an inner life, personal experiences, and responsibilities of her own. Sin occupies a position in *Paradise Lost* comparable to the position of Ignorance in *Pilgrim's Progress*, who, Carolynn Van Dyke argues, "exhibits in a particularly disturbing way the intermediary status of all Bunyan's agents": "Like Faithful, Christian, and the Mercie of Part II, he coincides at times with his idea, but he achieves thereby the opposite of transcendence. Although ontologically capable of changing to embody a good abstraction, he refuses to do so because, ironically, he firmly believes in human goodness. . . . Seeing no need for allegorical transformation, committed to the illusion of human self-sufficiency, he abdicates his autonomy as a human agent."[6] Bearing a name and shape that seem to identify her as an abstraction, Sin nevertheless has been charged with guarding the gates of Hell and endowed with the ability to reason about her conflicting duties to God and to her father and lover; although she perverts that reasoning, that she can reason implies that she is capable of right choice and redemption, even though she does not choose to change. It is the sense that she does not have any real choice or autonomy, that she cannot "fight allegorical destiny and win," that leads readers to dismiss the human aspect of her story. But it is only by insisting on a literal reading of Sin's conversation with Satan in Book 2 that Milton can use her as an example for his regenerate readers of how *not* to understand the workings of sexual hierarchy in their postlapsarian marriages.

Milton presents the relationship between Satan and Sin as a parody of marriage, an example of "unfit" partners and sinful mutuality. The interview at the gates of Hell, their first encounter after their fall, is an actual event, which plays a necessary role within the plot of the poem. During this mutual act of self-discovery, the couple reacquaint themselves with one another, catch up on what has happened, and grope their way toward a new understanding of their situation and of their relationship.

6. Van Dyke, *Fictions of Truth*, pp. 145–6, 184.

Sin recounts the horrible experience of giving birth to Death, telling Satan how the infant "breaking violent way / Tore through my entrails" (2.782–83). She recalls her fear, her futile flight, and the brutal rape with which Death begets the hellhounds. Now, she complains, her offspring "howle and gnaw / My bowels" and "with conscious terrours vex me round / That rest or intermission none I find" (2.799–802). Satan listens to her tale, considering how the information may be useful to him and what strategy may be most effective in assuring Sin's cooperation. He must develop a strategy for his dealings with Sin because she is not a one dimensional allegorical counter, like the figures in Spenser's parade of the Seven Deadly Sins, or a simple personification of evil, like Bunyan's Madam Bubble, but a psychologically complex being. She must be seduced to commit this sin.

The extremity of her plight leaves Sin, as a person, especially vulnerable to Satan's second seduction. He consoles her,

> Dear Daughter, since thou claim'st me for thy Sire,
> And my fair Son here shows't me, the dear pledge
> Of dalliance had with thee in Heav'n, and joys
> Then sweet, now sad to mention, through dire change
> Befall'n us unforeseen, unthought of, know
> I come no enemie.
>
> [2.817–22]

His speech satisfies her, for all its deep irony, because it seems to affirm her nostalgic memories of physical comfort and secret sexual joy in heaven as it reestablishes the terms of their relationship. The man who denied and rejected her now seems to recognize her claim on him. He speaks of "us" and promises protection. Continuing a pose he had first adopted during the Council in Hell, Satan casts himself as her redeemer, who comes to free her "From out this dark and dismal house of pain" (2.823). Parodying Christ's future sacrifice, Satan explains that he undertakes an errand in which he must "one for all / My self expose" (2.827–28) but which, if successful, will harrow Hell. He promises to

>   soon return
> And bring ye to a place where Thou and Death

> Shall dwell at ease, and up and down unseen
> Wing silently the buxom Air, imbalm'd
> With odours.
>
> [2.839–43]

Sensitive to Sin's psychology, Satan emphasizes physical ease and comfort in his seduction of her. His promise of unencumbered movement and a sweet atmosphere exploits the longings of a woman who experiences continuous physical pain, who must roll her heavy bulk awkwardly about her infernal home surrounded by the stench of her own festering body.

Satan, by casting himself as savior, or Christ, adopts the role that seventeenth-century pamphleteers considered appropriate for a husband to bear toward his wife. As John Bunyan advises, "When husbands behave themselves as husbands indeed, then will they be not only husbands, but such an ordinance of God to the wife, as will preach to her the carriage of Christ to his spouse. . . . 'For the husband is the head of the wife, even as Christ is the head of the church' Ep.v.23. and he is the Saviour of the body."[7] Sin's reply to Satan confirms at once the accuracy and the necessity of his seductive stratagems. She responds to Satan's suggestion of the obligations of their relationship rather than to her own physical needs, rationalizing her betrayal of the trust God has placed in her in terms of her dependence on and duty toward her husband. She explains that, while she holds the key to Hell "by due, / And by command of Heav'n's all-powerful King" (2.850–51), her duty to Satan is paramount. In words that Eve's speeches will soon echo, she declares,

> Thou art my Father, thou my Author, thou
> My being gav'st; whom should I obey
> But thee, whom follow?
>
> [2.864–66]

But her profession, unlike Eve's (cf. 4.440–43), denies any external referent to their relationship. Whereas Eve confirms her dependence on Adam in response to his evaluation of their

---

7. John Bunyan, *Of Christian Behavior,* in *Works,* 2: 558. See also Gouge, *Of Domesticall Duties,* for an elaboration of this analogy.

mutual obligations to God—"For we to him indeed all praises owe, / And daily thanks" (4.444–45)—Sin precedes hers with a bitter denial of the justice of God's sovereignty: "But what ow I to his commands above / Who hates me, and hath hither thrust me down[?]" (2.856–57). Like Satan, Sin denies her dependence on God and rejects her obligations to him, but unlike Satan, she recognizes the fact of his sovereignty. Considering herself a helpless pawn in the hands of a malevolent fate, Sin resigns herself to damnation, but a certain desperate recklessness accompanies her fatalism. Choosing to subordinate herself to Satan, who at least offers some temporary pleasure and comfort, Sin rationalizes her decision in terms that she believes absolve her of responsibility for her actions. She voices the subject's complementary remark to the tyrant's plea of necessity (4.393–94): Satan is her husband; he stands in relation to her as Christ does to his church. She must obey him.

Any careful reader who compares Sin's justification of her disobedience to God with the treatises on domestic duties current in Milton's time would realize that her reasoning is specious. The treatises argue that, though a woman owes even a bad husband or father obedience, she can never be constrained to act against her understanding of God's will. Because determining God's will in daily affairs can often be difficult, a woman must yield to her husband's will in "things indifferent" or in matters about which she is uncertain. As William Gouge writes, "Shee may do nothing against God's will; but many things must she doe against her owne will if her husband require her."[8] But in Sin's situation, the godly choice is clear.

Milton presents the scene as a burlesque of domestic rhetoric in which both Satan and Sin undercut their own arguments. Satan violates his responsibility to protect and instruct Sin by leading her deeper into damnation. Despite her extreme devotion to Satan's will, Sin fails to provide the spiritual and emotional solace that Milton identifies as the first end of marriage and primary responsibility of a wife. Their "marriage" does not fulfill the requirements Milton would demand of it. It seems a horrible perversion of God's promise to Adam:

8. Gouge, *Of Domesticall Duties*, p. 337.

> What next I bring shall please thee, be assur'd,
> Thy likeness, thy fit help, thy other self,
> Thy wish exactly to thy heart's desire.
>
> [8.449–51]

Satan responds to his first vision of Adam and Eve, "impara-
dised in one another's arms" (4.506), with envy and bitterness
over his own "fierce desire, / Among our other torments not the
least, / Still unfulfill'd with pain of longing" (4.509–11). Like
the apples that turn to ash in his mouth and aggravate his thirst
and hunger by their deception, Satan's "marriage" heightens
rather than cures his loneliness.

Sin's physical shape may provide a further gloss on her "marriage." She closely resembles the monstrous allegorical figure
Milton uses at the beginning of *The Doctrine and Discipline of
Divorce* to represent the inevitable union of custom with error:
"Custome being but a meer face, as Eccho is a meere voice, rests
not in her unaccomplishment, untill by secret inclination, she
accorporat her selfe with error, who being a blind and Serpentine body without a head, willingly accepts what he wants, and
supplies what her incompleatenesse went seeking" (*W* 3.368).
The monster's instruction, Milton writes, argues against reason, insisting, like Sin, on the letter rather than the spirit of the
law. Sin interprets marriage as an end in itself, rather than a
means to that "meet and happy conversation" that is conducive
to the worship of God and to the practice of charity (*W* 3.368).[9]
Using a rigid conception of her marital duties to abdicate moral
responsibility, Sin disguises her defiance of God as a submission to temporal authority. Her mistaken logic is precisely that
adopted by Eve after her fall to justify her separation from Adam
and to absolve herself of responsibility for her surrender to
Satan's temptations. Milton presents this parody of domestic
order to provide a corrective to the reader's possibly inappropriate response to the separation colloquy between Adam and Eve

---

9. See Gladys J. Willis, *The Penalty of Eve: John Milton and Divorce* (New
York: Peter Lang, 1984), for a discussion of the relationship between Milton's
theory of marriage as expressed in *The Doctrine and Discipline of Divorce* and
the Augustinian doctrine of charity.

in Book 9, the conversation that precedes their fall and becomes the focus of their contention after it.

III

After the Fall, Adam will accuse Eve of willful disobedience in having "wandered" from his side. Eve will counter his accusation with one of her own: "why didst not thou the Head / Command me absolutely not to go [?]" (9.1155–56). Adam's reply, while vicious and self-deluding, contains a kernel of sound correction. He speaks for Milton's higher conception of companionate marriage when he asks,

> what could I more?
> I warn'd thee, I admonish'd thee, foretold
> The danger, and the lurking Enemie
> That lay in wait; beyond this had bin force,
> And force upon free will hath here no place.
> [9.1170–74]

He repeats the declaration he made upon her departure, that a true marriage requires freedom of choice and mutual consent. Adam defends himself from responsibility for Eve's failure with the same logic that God uses to prevent questions about the fall of the bad angels and the fall of man, which he foresees. God declares, "I made him just and right, / Sufficient to have stood, though free to fall" (3.98–99), and asks, "Not free, what proof could they have giv'n sincere / Of true allegiance, constant Faith or Love [?]" (3.103–4). God desires not only love and obedience from his creatures but that their love be spontaneous and sincere. As Diane McColley explains, in *Paradise Lost* "obedience is not a following of a set of instructions but a response to a divine calling, made in one's own distinctive way."[10] Although Adam stands in relation to Eve as God to his creatures, he cannot force her to obey.

Milton defines marriage, instituted at the Creation, as "a

10. McColley, *Milton's Eve*, p. 56.

cov'nant the very beeing wherof consists, not in a forc't co-habitation, and counterfet performance of duties, but in un-fained love and peace" (*W* 3.400).[11] The love must be mutual and the exercise of obedience genuine and thoughtful. The pre-lapsarian relationship between Adam and Eve expresses this ideal. Adam praises Eve's

> words and actions mixt with Love
> And sweet compliance, which declare unfeign'd
> Union of Mind, or in us both one Soule.
> [8.602–5]

Eve first appears leaning on Adam; her hair, covering her like a veil, reminds the poet of the curling tendrils of a vine, "which impli'd / Subjection, but requir'd with gentle sway, / And by her yielded, by him best received" (4.308–9). Her loving assent to Adam's decisions about their activities expresses her own un-derstanding of their natures. Their relationship depends on a delicate balance of will, on Adam's loving authority and Eve's gracious obedience and cheerful assent. To defend himself from responsibility for Eve's fall, Adam simply reminds Eve of what she has always known.

Committed to presenting women as morally independent and responsible beings, Milton must invent a situation that allows Adam and Eve to separate innocently yet *deliberately*. He composes a scene in which disagreement evolves out of admirable motives and tender feelings. In the separation collo-quy, Eve suggests that she and Adam garden separately not because she wishes to be independent of Adam but because she is concerned that they distract each other from the work at hand. Adam himself praises Eve's desire to fulfill God's com-mand to dress the Garden but corrects her confusion of the

11. For a full discussion of Milton's position in relation to the Puritan doc-trine of marital love, see Haller and Haller, "The Puritan Art of Love"; A. G. George's chapter "The Top of Speculation: Man Embraces Woman," in *Milton and the Nature of Man* (New York: Asia, 1974); and Halkett, *Milton and the Idea of Matrimony.* Jean H. Hagstrum, *Sex and Sensibility: Ideal and Erotic Love from Milton to Mozart* (Chicago: University of Chicago Press, 1980), discusses Milton's contribution to the modern conception of married love.

means with the end of their obedience: God gave man work to dignify man, not to keep down vegetation. In an attempt to keep her with him, Adam reminds Eve, truthfully but not diplomatically, of her subordinate position in their relationship:

> leave not the faithful side
> That gave thee being, still shades thee and protects.
> The Wife where danger or dishonor lurks,
> Safest and seemliest by her Husband stays,
> Who guards her, or with her the worst endures.
>
> [9.267–69]

Eve, who values herself highly in proportion to Adam's admiration for her, is quite understandably hurt by his suggestion that her faith and love are not firm. Now needing to assert her sufficiency as an independent moral agent, she reminds Adam of his own arguments after her disturbing dream:

> Evil into the mind of God or Man
> May come and go, so unapprov'd, and leave
> No spot or blame behind.
>
> [5.117–19]

She reminds Adam that "harm precedes not sin" (9.327) and turns his argument against him.

McColley identifies Eve's argument in the separation colloquy as "Milton's argument for Christian liberty translated into prelapsarian terms": if she can't be trusted alone, then how "free" and sufficient is she? Adam, in response, argues the case for Christian responsibility: it is foolish to seek temptation. McColley believes that the colloquy concludes with Adam's blending of the two doctrines into a balanced expression of their freedom and faith.[12] But Adam's assent to Eve's position, while doctrinally correct, does not combine the two doctrines in a way that would enable Eve to remain by his side. After warning her, "Wouldst thou approve thy constancie, approve / First thy obedience" (9.367–68), Adam charges her,

12. McColley, *Milton's Eve*, p. 180.

Go; for thy stay, not free, absents thee more;
Go in thy native innocence, relie
On what thou hast of vertue, summon all
For God towards thee hath done his part, do thine.
[9.372–75]

Adam's statement precludes the possibility that her staying might be free. He places her in a double bind, for his conclusion requires her to choose between what Adam identifies as her own will and her obedience to Adam's, a false choice and one that she cannot make with impunity. It is precisely because of this double message that Milton writes that Eve "persisted, yet submiss" (9.375). Eve departs, "With thy permission then" (9.378), although independence and separation had not been her primary goal.

Although Eve's presence does not necessitate Adam's fall, she does embody the occasion for it. His sin will be to invert the proper hierarchy in his affections, choosing Eve instead of God; she herself will be the temptress. While Adam understands intellectually that Eve's suggestion that they garden separately arises from her desire to "best fulfil the work which here / God hath assigned us" (9.230–31), he indicates that his feelings have been hurt by suggesting another motive: "But if much converse perhaps / Thee satiate, to short absence I could yield" (9.247–48). This comment reveals the aptness of McColley's suggestion that "by stirring the passion that is Adam's 'good temptation' and the 'ingredient of vertu' he most needs to temper, Eve provides the challenge to Adam's 'manly grace / And wisdom' by which he chiefly grows."[13] Adam must continue to learn, as Raphael warned, not to attribute "overmuch to things / Less excellent" (8.565–66). Eve's ambiguous status as both an independent moral agent, responsible for her own rectitude, and as Adam's temptation complicates Milton's representation of her in this scene. Whereas Adam must temper his passion for Eve with well-considered self-esteem, she must temper her own self-confidence with a clear understanding of her subordinate status.

13. Ibid., p. 87.

Clearly Milton does not intend his readers to understand that Eve has sinned before she eats the fruit: her decision to leave Adam's side does not make her fall inevitable, nor does Adam abdicate his responsibility in letting her go. As McColley points out, Adam and Eve innocently separated and reunited earlier in the poem. But the consequences of this much-discussed separation convince both partners that Eve's decision to separate from Adam was wrong. Milton cannot get them apart in a deliberate and conscious way without creating a divergence of wills which is retroactively perceived as creating the occasion for the Fall. Although Eve departs "still sinless," the consequences of the Fall—the punishments the sinners receive, their reactions, and the terms of their reconciliation with one another—suggest that it was the independence of Eve's action, not just the sinfulness of it, for which she is guilty. Adam has sinned "against God only, I against God and thee" (10.931), not only by offering him the fruit but by leaving him in the first place. No matter how acceptable or important Eve's freedom may have been in prelapsarian Eden, the message to regenerate readers is clear.

Like Paul, Milton interprets the subordination of woman to man as a natural, or innocent, condition, exaggerated but not instituted by the Fall.[14] Given the Pauline understanding of human nature, the loving exercise of marital hierarchy is essential to piety because it preserves God's order: "But I would have you know, that the head of every man is Christ; the head of the woman is the man; and the head of Christ is God" (1 Cor. 11:3). Eve's early speeches to Adam express her own understanding of their relation. He is her Author and Disposer, Guide and Head:

14. Joseph Summers's chapter "The Two Great Sexes," in *The Muse's Method: An Introduction to "Paradise Lost"* (Cambridge: Harvard University Press, 1962), suggests that Milton intended a "separate but equal" understanding of Adam and Eve's relationship. Within the moral context of the poem, he points out, "nothing is self-sufficient and immutable except God" (p. 95), all creatures being adapted to fulfil themselves in relation to others. Diane McColley's article, "Free Will and Obedience in the Separation Scene of *Paradise Lost*," *Studies in English Literature* 12 (1972), argues that this hierarchical relationship does not restrict Adam and Eve but leaves them "free to act according to their nature, his in ruling justly and hers in yielding creatively." McColley believes that Eve's yielding, "though natural, is not necessary, for the purpose of the order of creation is voluntary love" (p. 111).

> what thou bidst
> Unargu'd I obey; so God ordains,
> God is thy law, thou mine.
>
> [4.635–37]

As scholars are quick to point out, Milton has very high expectations of marriage, and his ideas presuppose the value, dignity, and responsibility of the wife. In *The Doctrine and Discipline of Divorce*, Milton argues that the success of a marriage is secured by the wife's "fitness" for "the apt and cheerfull conversation of man with woman, to comfort and refresh him against the evill of solitary life," not just by her sexual fidelity (*W* 3.382). It is her responsibility to create a congenial home and be a "fit" partner. But in keeping with his Protestant contemporaries, Milton subordinates the well-being of the woman to the well-being of the man. Milton calls "Palpably uxorious!" the idea that divorce was instituted to relieve afflicted wives and asks, "Is it not more likely that God in his Law had more pitty towards man thus wedlockt, then towards the woman that was created for another [?]" His list of grounds for dissatisfaction focuses entirely on the comforts and needs of the husband: "What an injury is it after wedlock not to be belov'd, what to be slighted, what to be contended with in point of house-rule who shall be the head, not for any parity of wisdome, for that were somthing reasonable, but out of female pride" (*W* 3.475). Such an understanding of marital politics places an inordinate burden on the wife, for the only person capable of determining whether her attempts at house rule are appropriate or prideful is the husband. As the domestic treatises argue, a wife may challenge her husband's rule only when he asks her actively to disobey God; she must yield to his will in "things indifferent." Although Eve's departure in Book 9 arose from a conflict with Adam over "a thing indifferent," so that she could depart "still sinless," these arguments suggest that she should have chosen to stay.

Having sinned by eating the forbidden fruit, Eve becomes, like Sin, an idolatress of marriage. Because she worries about what Adam will now think of her and fears that she will lose him, she debates "in what sort / Shall I appear" (9.816–17) and

wonders whether to reveal what she has done. She seems to be
motivated by a newly discovered sense of inadequacy rather
than a desire to dominate, for she supposes that keeping this
knowledge secret may

> add what wants
> In Femal Sex, the more to draw his Love,
> And render me more equal.
> [9.821–23]

Although she finds this idea attractive, Eve does not forget the
probability that God will discover her disobedience and punish
her for it. Like Sin earlier, she now feels that God is remote and
hostile, "Our great Forbidder" (9.815). She realizes that her
death would mean her replacement with "another *Eve*," which
to her troubled mind seems "a death to think" (9.828, 830). No
longer secure in her relationship, she determines on a scheme
that will bind Adam to her: "*Adam* shall share with me in bliss
or woe" (9.831); she values the tree only as the means of holding
him.

Eve's possessive love for Adam perverts their marital relation
and renders her an "unfit wife" because her conversation no
longer contributes to Adam's spiritual welfare. Her speech to
Adam upon her return is excessively submissive but not, I
think, hypocritically so. She apologizes profusely for having left
his side and declares that "never more / Mean I to trie, what
rash untri'd I sought, / The pain of absence from thy sight"
(9.859–61). Desperately afraid of losing Adam, she herself views
her error as a desire for independence. She relates to him what
has happened—the transformation of the serpent, her own tasting of the fruit, and the fruit's heady effects. Stressing her courage and devotion, Eve claims that the fruit

> for thee
> Chiefly I sought, without thee can despise.
> For bliss, as thou hast part, to me is bliss,
> Tedious, unshar'd with thee, and odious soon.
> [9.877–80]

Casting herself in the dominant role, Eve offers herself as savior
to her husband, urging him to eat also of the fruit

> Least thou not tasting, different degree
> Disjoyne us, and I then too late renounce
> Deitie for thee, when Fate will not permit.
>   [9.883–85]

Her argument that they place their relationship above their responsibility to God clearly perverts what *Paradise Lost* defines as the end of marriage.

By affirming the inviolability of their bond, Adam, too, idolizes marriage. He exalts his love for Eve above his love for God, preferring alienation from God to the awful loneliness that he fears would haunt him even married to "another Eve." Reaffirming their union, he echoes his own words upon first seeing Eve:

> Flesh of my Flesh,
> Bone of my Bone thou art, and from thy State
> Mine never shall be parted, bliss or woe.
>   [9.914–16]

This time, however, the declaration reverberates with Eve's words, words with which, before her fall, she expressed her subordination:

> O thou for whom
> And from whom I was formd flesh of thy flesh,
> And without whom am to no end, my Guide
> And Head.
>   [4.440–43]

Coming from Adam, these words indicate the disorder of their relationship and the "effeminate slackness" into which he has fallen.

IV

When God, manifested in the Son, challenges Adam in the Garden, "Hast thou eaten of the Tree / Whereof I gave thee charge thou shouldst not eat?" (10.122–23), Adam acknowledges that his responsibility as a husband requires him to protect his dependent and weaker wife but claims that

> strict necessitie
> Subdues me, and calamitous constraint
> Least on my head both sin and punishment,
> However insupportable, be all
> Devolv'd.
>
> [10.131–35]

The whole blame, he feels, should fall on Eve, who, intended as his help, has proven defective. Although the Son replies that such an excuse will not serve, he rebukes Adam for his effeminacy, not for his evaluation of Eve. Adam, being superior, ought to have been governed by his own conscience. He errs in imagining Eve to be "Superior, or but equal, that to her / Thou did'st resigne thy Manhood" (10.147–48). Manly and eloquent in his own defense, Adam receives toil, sweat, and death as his punishment, but Eve, who is less articulate before God, not only shares Adam's punishment, she receives curses for herself as well. Because she has sinned against Adam as well as against God in perverting the marital hierarchy, Eve must submit herself more rigorously to her husband's rule. Her sexuality, the supposed solace of fallen humanity (9.1044), will subject her to pain in childbirth, a curse that promises to distort her body, as the births of Death and the hellhounds have distorted Sin's body.[15] Her newly developed sense of inadequacy, although it leads to idolatry of Adam and of marriage, is an attitude that Milton leaves uncorrected in the poem.

Adam blames Eve; Eve blames the serpent; and the serpent, helpless because mute, receives the most severe and most unjust punishment. Milton writes

> when the Lord God heard, without delay
> To Judgement he proceeded on th' accus'd
> Serpent though brute, unable to transfer
> The Guilt on him who made him instrument.
>
> [10.163–66]

15. For a discussion of seventeenth century statistics on and attitudes toward childbirth, see pp. 11–15.

The syntax of the passage purposely leaves unclear who is "unable to transfer" the guilt from the serpent to Satan, the serpent or the Son. Satan has fled. The Son in Heaven has declared that the fiend "best absent is condemn'd, / Convict by flight, and Rebel to all Law" (10.82–83); he then proceeds to condemn Satan in absentia. In treating this passage, Milton indicates in several ways his discomfort with the biblical text he has inherited. He has had the Son declare in Heaven that "Conviction to the Serpent none belongs" (10.84). While *conviction* may here refer to the serpent's sense of its own guilt as well as to its legal status,[16] the Son clearly states that the serpent ought not to be blamed for its part in the Fall: the idea of complicity cannot apply to a creature that has no reason, no freedom of choice, and no will. Yet in the Garden, as in Genesis, the Son does condemn the serpent. Milton's attempt to explain that the curse is actually meant for Satan, "Though in mysterious terms" (10.173), and his warning that "more to know / Concern'd not Man (since he no further knew) / Nor alter'd his offence" (10.169–71), do not resolve the problem. The unfortunate serpent is no mere proxy. The curse is inflicted on it also, and for all time. Milton, to justify the ways of his God, must condone and support this action: he argues that the serpent whom Satan has made

> instrument
> Of mischief, and polluted from the end
> Of his Creation [is] justly then accurst,
> As vitiated in Nature.
> [10.166–69]

The victim is guilty of having been victimized.

Like Sin and Eve, the serpent is created imperfect and then punished for it. Its condition prior to the Fall seems morally and sexually neutral. Raphael's description suggests the physical attributes but not the powers of the Medusa:

> Of huge extent somtimes, with brazen Eyes
> And hairie Main terrific, though to thee
> Not noxious, but obedient at thy call.
> [7.496–98]

16. See Alastair Fowler's footnote to this line in his edition of *Paradise Lost* (London: Longman, 1971), p. 511, which offers three possible interpretations for "conviction."

Its potential power lies dormant and pliant to command. But Satan, discovering it, considers the serpent "Fit Vessel, fittest Imp of fraud, in whom / To enter, and his dark suggestions hide" (9.89–90). Because of the serpent's natural "wit and native suttletie" (9.93), Satan believes that his presence will not alter its behavior as startlingly as it might some other beast's. The question seems to be whether this fitness of the serpent indicates some moral flaw within it. Satan finds the serpent sleeping, as he did Eve, but instead of simply whispering in its ear, Satan enters it through its mouth and possesses it. The entry is a kind of rape, for the sleeping serpent has no warning; it can neither consent nor resist.

Milton never suggests that the serpent erred in sleeping fearlessly in Eden and emphasizes its innocence before the Fall: "Nor nocent yet, but on the grassy herb / Fearless unfeared he slept" (9.186–87). The sleep indicates its vulnerability but also its innocence, for Milton, like Aristotle, believed that "sleep divests the mind of moral responsibility,"[17] an opinion he gives to Adam so that Eve might be reassured after her dream. The serpent becomes a figure of the woman, vulnerable, helpless, and curiously responsible for being so. The serpent completes the triad of Satan's instruments. Joining Sin, whom Satan seduces so that he may use her to get out of Hell, and Eve, whom he seduces so that he may use her to tempt Adam, the serpent embodies the extreme horror of the female condition: violated, used, and discarded, the serpent, unable to speak, unable to defend itself, must be punished for having been created incomplete.

As early as *Comus*, Milton explores this paradoxical quality of human nature in the context of female sexuality. There, the Elder Brother rebukes the Younger Brother's fears that his unguarded sister may be in physical danger in the forest. Chastity, the Elder Brother explains, is her defense: "She that has that is clad in compleat steel" (*C* 420). Her purity strikes even "brute violence / With adoration, and blank aw" (*C* 450–51). In fact, he argues, a true virgin is never really alone: "A thousand liveried

---

17. See Fowler's footnote, ibid., p. 259.

Angels lacky her / Driving far off each thing of sin and guilt" (*C* 454–55). She is not simply armed but armied. The influence of her heavenly companions refines the virgin's already pure soul "Till all be made immortal" (*C* 462). His theory sounds very much like the method Raphael says God planned for Adam and Eve in their ascent from Eden to Paradise had they not fallen. But, the Brother warns,

> when lust
> By unchaste looks, loose gestures, and foul talk,
> But most by leud and lavish act of sin,
> Lets in defilement to the inward parts,
> The soul grows clotted.
> [*C* 462–66]

Yet how, one might ask, does lust get in? What sparks these "leud and lavish" impulses? Clearly they derive from some internal flaw, some preexisting blemish "within." If lust cannot violate a truly chaste woman, armed with purity and attended by hosts of heavenly protectors, then any woman who experiences or is subjected to lust must not have been pure.

The allegory of Satan and Sin illustrates how thoroughly *Paradise Lost* locates this paradoxical quality of human nature in female sexuality. While Milton presents Sin's fallen condition as a graphic expression of the depth of Satan's degradation, this metamorphosis nevertheless disassociates sin from the male body. Sin's face, the part of her in which Satan views his perfect image, remains unchanged. She is still "woman to the waste, and fair" (2.650). Milton figures the deception and ugliness of sin in her deformed genitalia, which "ended foul in many a scaly fould / Voluminous and vast, as Serpent arm'd / With mortal sting" (2.651–53). As Sandra Gilbert has noted, the description of Sin's deformed body "seems to exaggerate and parody the female anatomy just as the monstrous bodies of Spenser's Error and Duessa do."[18] *Paradise Lost* offers no equivalent representation of male sexual deformity. Milton describes the annual humiliation of Satan and the devils in terms that

18. Gilbert, "Patriarchal Poetry," p. 373.

associate their serpentine forms with horrific women: the serpents cluster "thicker than the snaky locks / That curled Megaera" (10.560). They are subjected to the physical debasement of this "female" form only intermittently, while Sin's metamorphosis leaves her permanently Gorgon-bodied.

Before they fall, both Sin and Eve exhibit the awe-inspiring power of the Lady in *Comus*. When Sin bursts from Satan's forehead during the Council in Heaven, she seems "shining heav'nly fair, a Goddess arm'd" (2.757). She remembers that her person astonished the rebel council, for "amazement seis'd / All th' Host of Heav'n; back they recoild affraid" (2.758–59). Sin's effect resembles that of Minerva, her classical prototype, who sprang fully armed from the forehead of her father Zeus. As the Elder Brother explains, Minerva bore a "snaky-headed *Gorgon* sheild . . . / Wherwith she freez'd her foes to congeal'd stone" (*C* 446–48). Before her fall, Eve, too, resembles the Lady and the goddess Minerva. When she leaves the bower where Adam and Raphael are discussing cosmology,

> With goddess-like demeanour forth she went;
> Not unattended, for on her as queen
> A pomp of winning graces waited still,
> And from about her shot darts of desire
> Into all eyes to wish her still in sight.
> [8.59–63]

But while these graces shoot darts of desire, Eve's virtue seems to incorporate the power of Minerva's "rigid looks of Chast austerity" (*C* 449). When Satan discovers her, a week later, alone in the Garden, "her Heav'nly form / Angelic . . ."

> overawd
> His Malice, and with rapine sweet bereav'd
> His fierceness of the fierce intent it brought.
> [9.457–62]

Her presence, radiating active virtue like the sun, violates the integrity of Satan's evil: "That space the Evil one abstracted stood / From his own evil" (9.463–64), frozen like a person who has glimpsed the Gorgon shield, frozen as he was before the newborn Sin in Heaven.

One might suppose that Milton has placed Eve and Sin in opposition to one another in the scheme of imagery. Eve, like the Lady in *Comus*, is virtuous and pure, although her purity is expressed not as virginity but as matronly chastity. Sin, promiscuous and corrupted, resembles that other kind of woman mentioned in *Comus*. Her "attractive graces" (2.762) encourage rather than repel defilement. Satan overcomes his initial aversion to her, and their incestuous intercourse perverts her beauty: it transforms her from a Minerva figure, carrying the Gorgon image on a shield, to the Medusa herself. Milton seems to be playing with the opposition of Madonna and Harlot, but after her fall, Eve too becomes deformed in mind and body; she, too, becomes a Medusa.

Adam's response to Eve upon her return from the Tree of Knowledge indicates that her physical appearance has begun to reflect the distortion in her mind. The narrator remarks that "in her Cheek distemper flushing glow'd" (9.887). Adam "amaz'd, / Astonied stood and Blank, while horror chill / Ran through his veins, and all his joynts relax'd" (9.889–91). Eve no longer emanates virtue but inspires terror; the sight of her, like the sight of the Medusa, turns men to stone. As Milton did with Sin, he locates Eve's corruption in her sexuality: Adam exclaims, "How art thou lost, how on a sudden lost / Defac't, deflourd, and now to Death devote" (9.900–1). Her disobedience in accepting Satan disguised as the serpent as her guide, in listening to his reasoning, and in tasting the forbidden fruit has defiled her marriage bed. As Milton writes in *Of Christian Doctrine*: "Fornication signifies, not so much adultery, as the constant enmity, faithlessness, and disobedience of the wife, arising from the manifest and palpable alienation of the mind, rather than of the body" (W 15.179). Although Eve's sin has not been explicitly sexual, the perversion of her mind has polluted her body; after encouraging Adam to eat the fruit, she responds to his lust with equally immodest desire and bold eyes:

> hee on *Eve*
> Began to cast lascivious Eyes, she him
> As wantonly repaid.
> [9.1013–15]

Eve's eyes now dart "contagious fire" (9.1036), like the uncontrolled eyes of the Malecasta and Hellenore in *The Faerie Queene*. She no longer repels but attracts defilement.

v

During the separation colloquy, Adam warns Eve that God created man "secure from outward force; within himself / The danger lies, yet lies within his power" (9.343–49). In *Paradise Lost*, Milton separates this ambivalent aspect of internal frailty from man, figures it in the female, and then punishes her for it. Sin, unable to transcend her allegorical destiny, is punished for having embodied Satan's evil; despite her ambiguous ontological status, she is fully responsible for her actions. Eve, created to assuage Adam's need for fellowship and as an occasion for his exercise of godly nurturing and responsibility, is punished for having been created in need of guidance. For Milton, weakness is no excuse, because weakness reveals an inadequacy or flaw for which the flawed individual must take full responsibility. It is not only Milton's theological heritage that requires such a belief; in his time, a woman's complex social position richly reflected this dilemma, for traditional expectations of her response to her helplessness and subjection make her the natural embodiment of Christ as sacrifice, without his redemptive power.

Milton presents in Book 3 a model of harmonious marriage which is impossible for Eve to live up to. There, the Father offers the Son the problem of how to reconcile justice with mercy, to which the Son responds with "immortal love / To mortal men, above which only shone / Filial obedience" (3.267–69). The Son satisfies God's sense of justice by being perfectly selfless and obedient to the will of the Father, while responding to the problem with creative independence. But the distinction of persons within marriage differs drastically from the distinction of persons within the Trinity, for which marriage is only an accommodating metaphor. Raphael addresses the problem of accommodation before his attempt to describe the War in Heaven, warning Adam to remember that

> Immediate are the Acts of God, more swift
> Than time or motion, but to human ears
> Cannot without process of speech be told.
>   [7.176–78]

To accommodate Adam's inexperience and temporality, Raphael will speak as if the angels had human bodies and as if the "war" took place over time. Similarly, Milton presents the Father and the Son as two distinct characters in *Paradise Lost* because he needs to express an idea—the reconciliation of absolute justice with absolute mercy—dramatically. Although the Son plays the female complement to God the Father, he is also the image of God's masculine perfection. The perfect man, he transcends "man's effeminate slackness" by keeping his feminine qualities subordinate within himself.

Despite her admirable efforts toward reconciliation, Eve remains the scapegoat for Adam's guilt. When she humbles herself at his feet, admitting her "greater guilt," her posture and speech please Adam. It flatters and confirms his now corrected understanding of his own superiority to have her

> Now at his feet submissive in distress,
> Creature so fair his reconcilement seeking,
> His counsel whom *she* had displeas'd, his aid.
>   [10.942–44, italics mine]

Raising her to her feet, he dismisses her genuine offer of self-sacrifice as presumptuous and upstages it with a hypothetical one of his own. Eve, wondering that he accepts her "vile as I am" (10.971), suggests abstinence and starvation as means to limit their punishment. Although Adam had entertained those ideas himself, he can reject out of hand his own "temptations" because they are externalized in Eve. He can resist her suggestions as misguided attempts to usurp the dominant role in their marriage.

Eve speaks only fifty lines in the last two books of *Paradise Lost*. Silent and "much-humbl'd" (11.181), she retires at Adam's bidding when the archangel Michael approaches. He speaks only to Adam, save for a brief speech in which he admonishes Eve to accept her lot:

> Lament not *Eve*, but patiently resigne
> What justly thou hast lost; nor set thy heart,
> Thus over-fond, on that which is not thine;
> Thy going is not lonely, with thee goes
> Thy Husband, him to follow thou art bound.
>   [11.286–91]

Michael has been sent to "reveale / To *Adam* what shall come in future dayes" (11.113–14). He seals Eve's eyes that she may "sleep below while [Adam] to foresight wak'st" (11.368). At the close of Adam's instruction, Michael teaches him of the coming of Christ and the salvific nature of his sacrifice, so that Adam accepts Christ as his redeemer (12.572–73).[19] His act of faith achieves for him not only consolation, but "A paradise within [him], happier far" (12.587) than the one he loses. Eve does not reach this state within the poem. Michael leaves it to Adam to tell her "what may concern her Faith to know" (12.599), apparently because her dreams have been inspecific. They have, however, been successful. She wakes "compos'd / To meek submission" (12.596–97). Upon Adam's return, Eve expresses her willingness to go with him, "Who for *my* wilful crime art banisht hence" (12.619, italics mine). Adam hears "well-pleas'd, but answer'd not" (12.625). Although Milton describes Adam's response in words that resemble God's words of approval at Christ's baptism (Luke 3:22), Adam's silence fractures the echo. Eve's sacrifice mirrors that of the Son, but only faintly. Her submission and obedience satisfy Adam's sense of justice but cannot restore the marriage to its prelapsarian state. Adam, who is only human, does not offer her the praise or assurance that would reestablish their relationship on a more equal footing. Such a redemptive harmony of will is only possible within the perfect reciprocity of the divine couple, where the Son, in whom "all his Father shone / Substantially express'd" (3.140), responds perfectly and spontaneously to God's unexpressed will.

19. Mary Ann Radzinowicz, "Man as Probationer of Immortality," in *Approaches to "Paradise Lost,"* ed. C. A. Patrides (London: Edward Arnold, 1968), confirms that the visionary final books allow Adam to return to the world "as a Christian, in his lifetime having been vouchsafed a foreknowledge of the redeemer" (p. 39). This knowledge, she suggests, frees Adam to act heroically in his exile from Eden.

3

From Christiana to Stand-fast: Subsuming the Feminine in *The Pilgrim's Progress*

Eleven years after Milton published the first edition of *Paradise Lost*, John Bunyan issued the first part of his own vision of post-Restoration Christian heroism, *The Pilgrim's Progress*. Although Milton and Bunyan were contemporaries and compatriots, their works mark their wide separation in educational background and social status. Milton, Latin Secretary to Parliament under the Puritan Protectorate, read widely in literature, theology, philosophy, history, and science in classical, Semitic, and European languages. Bunyan, a foot soldier in the Parliamentary Army, admits to having read only the Bible, Martin Luther on Galatians, and a few pious tracts. While Milton prays that his heavily allusive, subtle epic find "fit audience . . . though few" (*PL* 7.13), Bunyan addresses his allegory to a wide, poorly educated reading public. His advice on how to conduct one's life as a regenerate Christian is more specific than Milton's: it is easier to understand how to denounce the frivolities of Vanity Fair, as Christian and Faithful do, than to figure out how to balance one's love of God and one's love for one's spouse, as Adam and Eve are asked to do. Bunyan argues that life is much simpler than Milton imagines: in *Paradise Lost*, Adam fails to sustain the appropriate balance between his love of God and his passion for Eve; in *The Pilgrim's Progress*, Christian rejects his family's entreaties by simply putting his fingers in his ears and running away.

Because Milton believes that women can exercise Christian heroism, although within a restricted sphere, he presents a complex portrait of the spiritual and emotional dynamics of the first human marriage. In contrast, Bunyan's married hero and heroine appear together only on the first three pages of Part 1. He is less interested in exploring the delicate balance of marital hierarchy than in insuring its broad outlines. Even in Part 2 of *The Pilgrim's Progress*, which focuses on the journey of Christian's wife Christiana, Bunyan is more interested in the female experience of marital subordination as a metaphor for male spirituality than he is in either marriage or female spirituality for its own sake. Bunyan's firm belief in the social and spiritual inferiority of women requires that he restrict the heroic activity available to Christiana until her story can no longer sustain his attention. In structuring *The Pilgrim's Progress*, Bunyan explicitly subsumes female experience and conventional virtues into the male ideal, an appropriation only latent in the role of the Son in *Paradise Lost* and *Paradise Regained*.

Bunyan published the story of Christiana's pilgrimage, Part 2 of *The Pilgrim's Progress*, in 1684, six years after his account of her husband Christian's journey toward salvation. Within the framing device of the dream-vision, which presents the dream as a text to be interpreted, both parts describe that journey literally: each pilgrim leaves the City of Destruction and proceeds on foot toward the Celestial City, but though Christiana also enters at the wicket gate, following the way Christian had traveled before her, her experience of the journey differs radically from his. Christian fled the City of Destruction suddenly and alone; Christiana finds time to pack before she sets out with her four sons and her neighbor Mercy. Her pace is far more relaxed: the course that Christian felt compelled to run in a few brutal days takes Christiana and her family many years. Unlike Christian, who travels through a lonely, confusing, and hostile landscape, Christiana and her family secure Mr. Great-heart to guide and instruct them, are welcomed into several Christian communities with which Christian has no contact, and find themselves in an ever-increasing company of fellow believers. In Part 2 of *The Pilgrim's Progress*, Bunyan's interest shifts from the desperate flight of the sinner to the more leisurely progress of the church fellowship,[1] from the individual to the family, from the male to the female.

Beginning with U. Milo Kaufmann's *"Pilgrim's Progress" and Traditions in Puritan Meditation*, discussion of *The Pilgrim's Progress* has focused on the rhetoric of progress. Kaufmann exposes a critical tension between the sudden completeness of a Christian's divinely accomplished salvation and the narrative unfolding of his "progress" toward it.[2] Stanley Fish suggests that the spiritual content of the allegory purposely undercuts the *"illusion* of a progress" created by the narrative. He discovers in the narrative itself a cyclic repetition of the Christian's static spiritual inadequacy, which repeatedly invalidates the individual's sinful confidence in "the metaphor of the journey,"[3] in the efficacy of his own efforts. Countering Fish, John Knott identifies "a progression through stages of spiritual life" in which the Christian, growing in grace and faith, learns that "the claims of the way and those of the world are mutually exclusive." Knott places Part 2 of *The Pilgrim's Progress* within the context of this discussion, arguing that "Christiana follows the same way that Christian does, though her temptations differ in degree from his, because Bunyan believed that patterns could be found in Puritan spiritual life."[4] But while Christiana's journey conforms to the pattern of spiritual progress established in Part 1, her experience of the Way

1. See John R. Knott, Jr., "Bunyan and the Holy Community," *Studies in Philology*, 80 (Spring 1983): 200–25, for a comprehensive discussion of Bunyan's concern with church community and the workings of a Separatist congregation.

2. U. Milo Kaufmann, *"The Pilgrim's Progress" and Traditions in Puritan Meditation* (New Haven: Yale University Press, 1966), pp. 107–17.

3. Stanley Fish, "Progress in *The Pilgrim's Progress,*" *English Literary Renaissance* 1 (1971): 265, 271 (reprinted in *Self-Consuming Artifacts* [Berkeley: University of California Press, 1972]).

4. John R. Knott, Jr., "Bunyan's Gospel Day: A Reading of *The Pilgrim's Progress,*" *English Literary Renaissance* 3 (1973): 448, 451, 449 (reprinted in his *The Sword of the Spirit: Puritan Responses to the Bible* [Chicago: University of Chicago Press, 1980]).

differs in kind as well as in degree from Christian's because Christiana is not, like her husband, a representative believer but a representative *female* believer

Christiana's sex determines both the nature of her journey toward salvation and the quality of her response to her call, her struggles, and her later effacement as "a mother in Israel." In Part 1, Bunyan expresses Christian's relationship to God as that of subject to king, his virtue as loyalty, and his sin as treason. He challenges the fiend Apollyon, for example: "I have given him [God] my faith, and sworn my allegiance to him; how then can I go back from this, and not be hanged as a traitor?" (91). Bunyan reconceives this metaphor before applying it to Christiana, displacing it from the political to the domestic sphere. He presents Christiana's relationship to God as that of Bride to Bridegroom, modeling her journey on the searchings of the Bride in the Song of Solomon. In developing this relationship, he represents female virtue as chastity within marriage[5] and female sin as sexual misconduct, taking the forms of adultery, promiscuity, prostitution, and even being raped. But unlike the Bride, who remains admirable despite her wanderings and "undefiled" even though she has been attacked by watchmen who "took away my veil from me" (Song 5:7), Christiana's encounter with "two very ill-favoured ones" radically alters her experience of the way and prevents her from retaining her role as *ecclesia* and bride. She becomes simply a mother in Israel, a female believer within the church, because Bunyan's belief in the spiritual inferiority of women makes it impossible for him to assign positive allegorical significance to a female character.

Like Milton, Bunyan derives his understanding of female insufficiency from Puritan doctrine, which bases its domestic theory on the Pauline declaration that "the husband is the head of the wife, even as Christ is the head of the church" (Eph. 5:23). William Gouge explains that "a familie is a little Church" and identifies "the end why an husband is appointed to be the head

---

5. See Hill, *World Turned Upside Down*. Hill's chapter "Base Impudent Kisses" discusses both the Puritan concept of female chastity within marriage and Bunyan's reaction against the freedom allowed women in the emerging Protestant sects.

of his wife, namely that by his provident care he may be as a saviour to her."[6] In *Of Christian Behaviour*, Bunyan clarifies this point, writing that "when husbands behave themselves like husbands indeed, then will they be not only husbands, but such an ordinance of God to the wife, as will preach to her the carriage of Christ to his spouse."[7] Christiana's spiritual security can only be assured within the context of her marriage to Christian or, now that he is dead, within a congregation supervised by men. As a second-class believer, she cannot adequately represent universal Christian experience.

From the beginning of her pilgrimage, Christiana's wifehood mediates and defines her relationship to God. The first workings of grace in her soul manifest themselves as loneliness and guilt over the loss of her husband, whereas Christian discovers his sinfulness while reading a book that warns him to "fly from the wrath to come" (41): he abandons his wife and children, stopping his ears against their cries. Christiana blames her spiritual crisis on "all her unkind, unnatural, and ungodly carriages to her dear friend," crying to her children, "Sons, we are all undone. I have sinned away your father" (223). Christiana's response conforms to Puritan conflation of a woman's marital and spiritual responsibilities. As Bunyan's contemporary Benjamin Wadsworth writes, a wife who behaves badly toward her husband "not only affronts her husband, but also God her Maker, Lawgiver and Judge, by this wicked behaviour. The indissoluble Authority, the plain Command of the Great God, requires Husbands and Wives, to have and manifest very great affection, love and kindness to one another."[8] John Milton's definition of *fornication*—"not so much adultery, as the constant enmity, faithlessness, and disobedience of the wife, arising from the manifest and palpable alienation of the mind, rather than of the body" (*W* 15.179)—seems particularly perti-

---

6. Gouge, *Of Domesticall Duties*, pp. 18, 30.

7. Bunyan, *Of Christian Behavior*, in *Works*, 2:558. Subsequent references to Bunyan's nonfiction prose will be made by volume and page number in the text.

8. Benjamin Wadsworth, *The Well-Ordered Family* (Boston, 1712), Evans American Bibliography, Catalogue #1591, pp. 25–26.

nent to Christiana's spiritual situation. Just as Milton's Eve confesses after her fall that "both have sinn'd, but thou / Against God only, I against God and thee" (*PL* 10.930–31), Christiana recognizes that her domestic failings jeopardize her salvation.

Bunyan presents Christiana's conviction of sin in terms of her role as estranged wife. It begins with her dream in which "the times, as she thought, looked very black upon her" (224); two "very ill-favoured" men discuss preventing her pilgrimage; and her husband appears in "a place of bliss among many immortals" (224), a place that seems inaccessible to her. The next morning, Christiana receives a messenger to whom she responds as a woman would to a messenger from her lover; she "blushed and trembled, also her heart began to wax warm with desires to know whence he came, and what was his errand to her" (225). The messenger does come from Christiana's lover, or, more correctly, from her lovers. He brings a perfumed letter from her husband's king, who asks her to "do as did Christian her husband; for that was the way to come to his City, and to dwell in his presence with joy forever" (225). Just as Bunyan defines Christiana's sin in terms of her duty to her husband, blaming her for "the evil thou hast formerly done to thy husband in hardening thy heart against his way" (225), he presents her future happiness as a reunion with Christian. Christiana exhorts her children to "pack up, and be gone to the Gate that leads to the Celestial Country, that we may see your father and be with him and his companions in peace" (226). For Christian, as Stanley Fish notes, "the claims of 'Eternal Life' are made at the expense of this life—its pleasures, its values, its loyalties."[9] But Christiana's spiritual crisis initiates a journey toward completion in fellowship. She conflates her union with God with her reunion with Christian, for her husband, as the head of their spiritual body, acts as God's representative to her.

Mercy's relationship to God mirrors Christiana's as an engagement mirrors a marriage. Mercy is both New Testament virgin and Old Testament handmaiden. She identifies her fears at being left outside the gate in the terms of the parables of

9. Fish, "Progress," p. 274.

election: "Now thought I, 'tis fulfilled which is written, *Two women shall be grinding together; the one shall be taken, and the other left*" (238). The Interpreter compares her to Ruth, "who did for the love that she bore to Naomi, and to the Lord her God, leave father and mother and the land of her nativity to come out and go with a people that she knew not heretofore" (255). Bunyan does not explicitly press the typological possibilities of the Ruth-Boaz story, but he works into his portrait of Mercy a remarkable number of parallels to it, details that reveal his inevitable categorizing of spiritual experience by gender. Like Ruth, Mercy follows a widowed older woman on her journey to her homeland out of love for her. Like Ruth, who asks, "Why have I found grace in thine eyes, that thou shouldest take knowledge of me, seeing I *am* a stranger?" (Ruth 2:10), Mercy fears Christ's rejection, because "I am come, for that unto which I was never invited" (236). Like Ruth, who asks Boaz for permission to glean in his fields and later for his protection in marriage, Mercy desires that "if there is any grace and forgiveness of sins to spare, I beseech that I thy poor handmaid may be partaker thereof" (237). Both young women are accepted for their virtuous devotion; their marriages, arranged by their mothers-in-law, insure the continuance of God's chosen people (315, Ruth 4:10).

As they journey toward salvation, the women encounter obstacles and receive instruction appropriate to their sex. Mrs. Timorous attempts to dissuade Christiana from the journey by accusing her of "unwomanly" behavior. She appeals to Christiana's duty to her children—"Pray, for your poor children's sake, do not so unwomanly cast away yourself"—and to her vulnerability—"For if he, though a man, was so hard put to it, what canst thou, being but a poor woman, do?" (227, 228).[10] A

---

10. Christiana's neighbors, failing to keep her at home, express their irritation at her higher apprehension of "wifely duty" with slander and gossip. They gossip about carnal pleasures and what the domestic theorists of the time would consider inappropriate and irresponsible behavior for married women: "I was yesterday at Madam Wanton's, where we were as merry as the maids. For who do you think should be there, but I, and Mrs Love-the-flesh, and three or four men, with Mr Lechery, Mrs Filth, and some others. So there we had music and dancing and what else was meet to fill up the pleasure" (231).

barking dog frightens the women when they approach the wicket gate. This domestic threat of violence replaces the archers on the ramparts of the adjacent castle, who attempt to keep Christian from entering the Way alive.[11] Christian transgresses actively before he reaches the gate, turning out of the Way at the advice of Mr. Worldly Wise-man (50–51). It is Christian's breach of allegiance to God. In mute rebellion, he decides to go to live in the village of Morality, rather than to continue on to the Celestial City. But the transgression is also appropriate to the nature of Christian's sinfulness: his burden wearies him, so he goes to have it removed. Noting the differences between Christian's and Faithful's trials, Fish remarks that "the perils of the way are generated by a pilgrim's weakness, and they persist as long as it persists."[12] A man's "burden," or particular human weakness, creates the occasion for and determines the kind of sin he will commit.

Christiana, however, passively suffers her first and only transgression, a transgression that appropriately threatens her relationship to God as it conforms to the nature of her own sinfulness. As a woman, she carries her sin, the "burden" of her sexuality, within her; therefore, Bunyan represents her transgression as an attempted rape by "two ill-favoured ones." Although the men at first try to seduce Christiana and Mercy, their persistence, even as the women kick and cry out "murder," indicates that they do not require compliance to accomplish their ends. Bunyan's injustice in equating rape with sexual temptation and spiritual pollution is so commonplace as to be quite unperceived by him: he simply causes Christiana, who has been well socialized, to make that identification herself. Neither Bunyan nor his seventeenth-century audience could find her admirable unless she interpreted her experience in this way. Resisting the would-be rapists, she says, "We will rather die upon the spot than suffer ourselves to be brought into such snares *as shall hazard our well-being hereafter*" (242, emphasis mine). She radically identifies physical with spiritual weakness

---

11. See Lynn Veach Sadler, *John Bunyan* (Boston: Twayne, 1979), p. 101.
12. Fish, "Progress," p. 266.

and believes, as will Richardson's Clarissa, that a violation of her physical integrity, no matter what the circumstances, corrupts her soul.

Bunyan insists throughout *The Pilgrim's Progress* on the dangers for women of social and spiritual independence. The man who rescues Christiana and Mercy marvels, "being that ye knew ye were but weak women, that you petitioned not for a conductor" (243). Christiana attempts to assign the blame for her predicament to God's negligence, arguing that "since our Lord knew 'twould be for our profit, I wonder he sent not one along with us" (243). Her rescuer retorts that "it is not always necessary to grant things not asked for lest by doing so they become of little esteem" (243). He explains that the incident is a kind of lesson, for "had my Lord granted you a conductor, you would neither so have bewailed the oversight in not asking for one as now you have occasion to do" (243). But at the beginning of her journey, Christiana did request that the messenger Secret accompany her to the Celestial City and was refused with an admonition that contradicts the Reliever's claim that the Lord would have granted them a guide: "Christiana! The bitter before the sweet! Thou must through troubles as did he that went before thee enter the Celestial City" (226). Neither Bunyan nor Christiana now mentions the initial request or acknowledges the inherent contradiction between the two incidents. Christiana simply confesses her "folly" in traveling without a man.

This contradiction in the text reveals the conflicting nature of the two points Bunyan wishes to make: each individual believer must traverse the spiritual road alone, but female believers cannot be allowed spiritual independence. Bunyan must have Christiana ask for and be refused a guide to correct his readers' misapprehensions about the difficulty of the Way, but he must have her unsupervised journey end in near disaster to underscore for his female readers the danger of independence. Christiana's confession of error works on the allegorical level within the interpretive context of the dream, as well as on the literal, narrative level. In spiritual as in worldly matters, a woman must turn to men for guidance and protection. In *A Case of Conscience Resolved* (1683), Bunyan advises against segregated worship for women, claiming that "worship was ordained before woman was made, wherefore the word of God did not immediately come to her, but to him that was first formed, and made the head in worship" (2.665). Milton's Eve expresses her own spiritual incompleteness, when she addresses Adam as

>   thou for whom
> And from whom I was form'd flesh of thy flesh,
> And without whom am to no end, my Guide
> And Head.
>
>   [*PL* 4.440–43]

She then enacts the "truth" of her self-evaluation in her unsupervised excursion and fall. Gouge charges husbands to care for their wives "as Christ nourisheth and cherisheth his Church, not only with things temporall, but also with things spirituall and eternall," encouraging mutual prayer as a duty that "doth especially concern the husband, who is as a Priest unto his wife, and ought to be her mouth to God when they two are together." He warns darkly that "she who first drew man into sin, should be now subject to him, lest by like womanish weaknesse she fall again."[13] Where Christian must learn to rely on God's intervention for his success, Christiana must learn to rely on male protectors.

In the context of this belief in a woman's spiritual weakness, Christiana expresses her embarrassment and sense of guilt over having allowed herself to be sexually attacked. She immediately connects this incident with her earlier dream about "the two very ill-favoured ones," telling Mercy that "before I set foot out of doors, one night as I lay in my bed, I had a dream about this" and lamenting, "This you know might have made me take heed, and have provided when provision might a been had" (244). Mercy confirms Christiana's guilt over "this neglect" and sees the event as an occasion to "behold our imperfections" (244). Mercy has discovered her own vulnerability; her response to the sight of the three hanged rogues expresses the violent

13. Gouge, *Of Domesticall Duties*, pp. 79, 235, 269.

indignation of a potential victim: "Let them hang and their names rot . . . , who knows else what they might a done to such poor women as we are" (263). Neither does Christiana forget the "lesson" of her sexual assault. As she confesses to the Interpreter, the dream of the two ugly men

> hath troubled me much: yea, it still runs in my mind, and makes me afraid of everyone that I meet, lest they should meet me to do me a mischief, and to turn me out of the way. Yea, I may tell my Lord, tho' I would not have everybody know it, that between this and the Gate by which we got into the way, we were both so sorely assaulted, that we were made to cry out murder, and the two that made this assault upon us, were like the two that I saw in my dream. [254]

On the surface, Christiana expresses the understandable paranoia of a victim of violent attack; her reluctance to speak of her sexual assault reveals the extent of her socialization: she is ashamed to have been sexually attacked and would keep her experience a secret. She accepts society's assignment to the victim of the guilt for rape. Although she covered herself with her veil, she believes that she tempted the two men. Such a response would have been reinforced in Puritan circles by sermons that located temptation and desire within women and rigorously defined behavior appropriate to a Christian woman: "Careful she likewise is, lest hereby she deceive unwary men into those Amours which bewitching looks and smiles do often betray the Children of men, especially those that are *but* Children of men, into."[14] But on a deeper level, Christiana interprets the fear that these two men symbolized in her dream as an expression of suppressed desire. She, after all, had learned of this danger before she left home; reading retrospectively, she assumes that the men's presence in her dream must have been a warning she willfully ignored. The spiritual and physical aspects of the rape experience coalesce: Christiana worries that she wants to be kept from salvation, that she wants to be raped.

14. Cotton Mather, "Ornaments for the Daughters of Zion" (Boston, 1692), Evans American Bibliography, Catalogue #624, p. 12.

Christiana stays longer at the House of the Interpreter than Christian did, depending on the Interpreter to provide the spiritual instruction she cannot receive from her now dead husband. Although he shows her the significant rooms that Christian saw, the Interpreter tailors the bulk of his instruction to Christiana's sex. He shows the women and children scenes from nature and domestic life "because you are women, and they are easy for you" (249). After his short visit with the Interpreter, Christian loses his burden before the Cross. Christiana and Mercy do not have this experience, however, because their sin, being their sexuality and not a simple "burden," is within. They must be purified; so at this point in the journey, the women are given a ritual bath—what Bunyan glosses in the margin as "The Bath of Sanctification" (255). Innocent, a damsel in the Interpreter's household, tells them that "they must wash and be clean, for so her Master would have the *women* to do that called at His House as they were going on pilgrimage" (256, emphasis mine). The women, with Christiana's children, who, according to the practice of covenanted churches, are grouped with their parents until they are spiritually independent, wash in the Bath. They emerge "sweet," "clean," "enlivened," and "strengthened." They also look "fairer a deal than when they went out to the washing" (256).

Clearly Bunyan intends more by the Bath than a concession to the demands of his Baptist readers.[15] As recent critics agree, this incident cannot be precisely defined as either allegory or actual church practice.[16] Christiana and Mercy participate in a custom similar to the Jewish mikvah, the bath of purification required for women before marriage and after each menstrual period or pregnancy so that they may be "clean" for their husbands. That the children must also bathe connects Bunyan to the Augustinian understanding of Original Sin as sexually transmitted.[17] They must be purified from the contamination

15. See Monica Furlong, *Puritan's Progress: A Study of John Bunyan* (London: Hodder and Stoughton, 1975), p. 119.

16. See Knott, "Bunyan and the Holy Community," p. 217; and Van Dyke, *Fiction of Truth*, p. 191.

17. John Calvin cites Job 14:4—"Who can bring a clean thing out of an

of the birthing process. Mikvah survived in Christian tradition as the churching of women, a practice denounced in *The Admonition to Parliament* (1572) as legalistic and superstitious: "Churching of women after childbirth, smelleth of Jewish purification: theyr other rytes and customes in their lying in, & comming to church, is foolish and superstitious, as it is used."[18] But not all Puritans rejected the ceremony or its significance. The Puritan redactors of the prayer book omitted the churching of women in their 1578 edition but restored it again in 1589.[19]

Bunyan is not the only Puritan to have endowed this ritual of physical cleansing with spiritual significance. Milton refers to the custom in his sonnet "Methought I Saw My Late Espoused Saint," where he imagines his wife to have been both physically and spiritually cleansed of "child-bed taint" in death. (Milton uses mikvah as the type of Old Law purification for which he understands Resurrection to be the antitype under the New Law.) In *The Pilgrim's Progress*, this Bath of Sanctification, specifically designed for women, cleanses them of their fallen nature, of their impure sexuality, and prepares them to be Brides of Christ. Significantly, Christian's experience of sanctification does not involve immersion, and Bunyan argues strenuously in his religious tracts against the necessity of water baptism and against its status as a mystery or church ordinance.[20]

---

unclean? Not one"—to refute the idea that original sin "passed by imputation, not by propagation." He points out, "The orthodox, therefore, and more especially Augustine, laboured to show that we are not corrupted from acquired wickedness, but bring an innate corruption from the very womb" (*Institutes of the Christian Religion*, trans. Henry Beveridge, 2 vols. [Grand Rapids, Mich.: Wm. B. Eerdman, 1953], 1:214). Milton's description of how Sin will infect the human race suggests that original sin is a kind of venereal disease (*PL* 10.606–9).

18. *The Admonition to Parliament*, in *Puritan Manifestoes: A Study of the Origin of the Puritan Revolt, with a reprint of the Admonition to Parliament and kindred documents, 1572*, ed. W. H. Frere and C. E. Douglas (London: Society for Promoting Christian Knowledge, 1907), p. 28.

19. For a discussion of Puritan revisions to the prayer book, see Francis Proctor and Walter Frere, *A New History of the Book of Common Prayer* (London: Macmillan, 1961), pp. 133–34.

20. In "A Confession of My Faith, and A Reason of My Practice," Bunyan argues against water baptism as an initiating ordinance and a prerequisite to

The ceremony after the Bath closely parallels the events following Christian's loss of his burden. In Part 1, three Shining Ones approach Christian as he stands weeping for wonder and joy before the Cross: "The first said to him, 'Thy sins be forgiven.' The second stripped him of his rags, and clothed him with a change of raiment. The third also set a mark on his forehead" (70). The Interpreter sets a similar mark upon Christiana and Mercy and commands that raiment of fine white linen be given to them. But this adornment affects the women more powerfully than it did Christian. Bunyan writes that "this seal greatly added to their beauty . . . and made their countenances more like them of angels" (256). Clothed in their white garments, the women seem "to be a terror one to the other, for that they could not see that glory each one on herself which they could see in each other" (256). Purified and transformed, the women may now approach the Cross, where their guide, Great-heart, explains the salvific effects of the Crucifixion in terms of bathing and clothing: "He has performed righteousness to cover you, and spilt blood to wash you in" (258). Their double purification, first by physical immersion, then by the spiritual cleansing of the Crucifixion sacrifice, differs markedly from Christian's purely spiritual experience of sanctification.

As evidence of their spiritual reformation, Christiana and Mercy now place all their trust in male authority, which guides them, protects them, and instructs them in proper female conduct. Great-heart leads the women and children from the Cross to House Beautiful, slaying the Giant Grim on the way. The family rests at House Beautiful "a month or above" (274), delighting in the companionship of the holy women there. When Matthew gets a grippe, Christiana briefly accuses herself of negligence, but from this point on, nothing seriously disturbs the women's spiritual tranquillity. Mercy sews for the poor and

---

participation in the Lord's Supper (2:606). He distinguishes between baptism by water and baptism in the Spirit, referring to Paul's distinction between circumcision in the flesh and circumcision in the Spirit. In a later treatise, "Differences in Judgment about Water Baptism, No Bar to Communion" (1673), Bunyan challenges a critic of his reading of Ephesians 4:1–6 saying, "The sixth argument is, There is 'one baptism.' Now we are come to a pinch, viz., whether it be that of water, or no? which I must positively deny" (2:623).

marries, as she is directed, within the faith. Both women devote themselves to their children. The family passes safely through the Valley of Humiliation, which, appearing fruitful and pleasing to the women, suits Mercy's spirits (291), and through the Valley of the Shadow of Death. There, Great-heart challenges the Giant Maul and slays him, while the women and children watch, sighing and crying (297).

As the culmination of their instruction, the women learn from the innkeeper Gaius about their place within the scheme of salvation. He delivers a speech "on the behalf of women to take away their reproach," the reproach of their sexuality. Traditionally, "the reproach of women" refers to barrenness, such as that of Rachel, Michal, or Elizabeth, who became mother of John the Baptist. But barrenness is a "reproach" because it prevents women from participating in the one redemptive activity available to them, to produce offspring that they might repair the sin of their first mother. As Gaius explains, "For as death and the curse came into the world by a woman, so also did life and health" (316). He argues that, despite their sinful connection to Eve because of their sex, women "are sharers with us in the grace of life" (316), partly from scriptural examples of women ministering to Jesus and partly from 1 Timothy 2:14–15: "And Adam was not deceived, but the woman being deceived was in the transgression. Notwithstanding she shall be saved through childbearing, if they continue in faith and charity and holiness with sobriety." The woman's fertility, as well as her willing subordination to her believing husband, will mitigate the punishment Original Sin has imposed on her because of her sex. Marriage becomes a necessity for her. This consideration, as well as a strong belief in the Puritan concept of tribal sainthood, presumably influences Gaius's eagerness to marry off Mercy and his own daughter Phoebe.[21] That evening, the

21. Cotton Mather makes the same arguments for marriage and motherhood in *Ornaments for the Daughters of Zion* and in *Elizabeth in her holy Retirement*. Edmund Morgan notes the tribal nature of the Puritan vision of salvation, the belief that salvation can be physically inherited, in *The Puritan Family*. See also Stone, *Family, Sex, and Marriage*, p. 416, for the Puritan arguments that birth control would reduce the number of the Elect and that "childbirth brought honour to women and aided them to achieve salvation."

adults, Christiana, Great-heart, Gaius, and Old Honest, sit up until dawn, but Christiana, who now knows her place, listens "in silence with all subjection" (1 Tim. 2:11).

Barely halfway through his account of Christiana's pilgrimage, Bunyan's emphasis switches from Christiana and her family to the larger experience of male believers. Immediately after Great-heart's victory over the Giant Maul, the family discovers an old gentleman asleep under an oak. After praising Christiana for her husband's exemplary faith and blessing her boys, Old Honest converses with Great-heart about the pilgrimages of Mr. Fearing and Mr. Self-will. It is true that these stories, as Knott argues, are "object lessons" for the pilgrims and the reader, offering a rich variety of spiritual models,[22] but Bunyan multiplies these secondhand histories because he has exhausted the range of spiritual experience his ideology will allow women. Because Bunyan restricts his female characters to real-life roles, he must rely on male activity to move the group along the road, to offer protection, and to provide dramatic interest.

During the remainder of *The Pilgrim's Progress*, Christiana and Mercy mend clothes while the men slay giants. The men launch three expeditions. Near the inn, they rescue Mr. Feeble-mind from the Giant Slay-good. At Vanity Fair, they join the elders of the gathered congregation there to engage the Babylonian monster, although with small success; at By-path stile, they leave the women in the road while they storm Doubting Castle. Christiana and Mercy provide the music at the victory celebration; Christiana, in accordance with her role as mother, revives the starving Mr. Despondency with food and medicinal spirits. The company, for it can hardly be called a family any longer, proceeds like an army on maneuvers, with a small camp following of women and children, although the littlest ones are left with a shepherd this side of the Delectable Mountains; like a volunteer army, it continues to swell. Mr. Valiant-for-truth, a proper militant with a fine Jerusalem blade, joins up shortly after the Delectable Mountains; they find Mr. Stand-fast at prayer in the midst of the Enchanted Ground.

Bunyan does not pay much attention to Christiana or Mercy

22. Knott, "Bunyan and the Holy Community," p. 209.

between the House Beautiful and the Land of Beulah. They have each "risen a mother in Israel" (268), to be noticed and praised only for their husbands and sons (see 301, 331, 351). Mercy, who fell in love with her salvation through Christiana's influence (232), following her out of a love as strong as Ruth's for Naomi (255), becomes simply "Mercy the wife of Matthew" (344), "a young, and breeding woman" (345). Bunyan speaks of her as if the reader would not remember who she was: her wifehood subsumes her past and personality. More strikingly, he diminishes the strength of the bond between the two women. When Christiana gathers the company around her deathbed, she has no special token for this dear daughter. She simply remarks on the signs of chastity in all her daughters-in-law, the marks on their foreheads and their snowy garments; but recognizing her spiritual kinship to Stand-fast, she gives him her ring, the symbol of her chastity toward her husband and toward God (366).

Although he has restricted Christiana's role in the last half of Part 2 to that of concerned mother and submissive churchwoman, Bunyan describes her death in detail, stressing her femininity and her love relation with the Lord. Christiana is the first of her band of pilgrims to be called over the river. The message from her Lord again comes in the form of a letter, which begins like the annunciation of Mary, "Hail, good woman" (365). As an assurance that the call is genuine, Christiana receives a love token from her Bridegroom—"an arrow with a point sharpened with love [that] let easily into her heart" (365). All the male pilgrims who die receive only passages of Scripture as assurance of their calls. The love-poisoned arrow, which prepares Christiana to die, suggests that her death will consummate her marriage to Christ, although Bunyan predictably avoids using the word *die*.

But Bunyan does not close Part 2 of *The Pilgrim's Progress* with Christiana's death. Seven more pilgrims cross over the river to the Celestial City before Bunyan bids his reader adieu. The last of them is Stand-fast, whom the group found praying on the Enchanted Ground. Like Christiana, Stand-fast has resisted persistent sexual advances. When he relates his ordeal, however, Stand-fast is not chastised for having encouraged Madam Bubble or having secretly desired her "enticements"

(361). Because Bunyan locates sexual lust firmly within the female, Great-heart condemns Madam Bubble as "a bold and impudent slut" (362), displacing his anger at lust onto the woman. She has become a personification of sexual evil and functions as a scapegoat, bearing on her head all the sins of the world (363). Bunyan, who identifies Christiana's attackers as a projection of her own carnal desires, glosses Madam Bubble as "this vain world" (361); Stand-fast is not responsible for his own attraction to it. The female body represents earthly imperfection. Women may be cleansed of their sexual evil, but they cannot divest themselves of their womanly bodies. In a system where man corresponds to woman as spirit to flesh, however, male characters can transcend the taint of sexuality.

Although he has established the Christian's metaphorical relationship to God as beloved to lover within the normal sexual nexus, Bunyan, in the tradition of Christian devotional literature, transfers the metaphor to the male. He appropriates for his hero Stand-fast distinctly feminine language, language that in the logic of the allegory belongs in Christiana's mouth. Stand-fast, wearing Christiana's ring, rejoices in the person of the male Beloved, Christ, as he anticipates their union: "His name has been to me as a civet-box, yea, sweeter than all perfumes. His voice to me has been most sweet, and his countenance I have more desired than they that have most desired the light of the sun. His words I did use to gather for my food, and for antidotes against my faintings" (372). Stand-fast's magnificat employs the richly sensuous imagery of the Song of Solomon. His final sentence, "Take me, for I come unto thee" (373), transforms his death into an explicitly sexual surrender. In this moment, Bunyan completes the displacement of the female implicit in the controlling metaphor of the second part. Whereas in *Paradise Lost* the Son's feminine subordination to the Father offers Eve a model for her own Christian heroism, in *The Pilgrim's Progress*, Bunyan's transfer of the role of the Bride of Christ to Stand-fast excludes Christiana and all other women from that role. Stand-fast, the male perfection of the idea of the feminine, usurps Christiana's role. The type of a "higher chastity"—male chastity—Stand-fast can become the most perfect Bride of Christ.

4

Most Happy Punishment: The Sanctification of Clarissa

I

Samuel Richardson began publishing his four-volume epistolary novel *Clarissa* in 1747, sixty years after Bunyan published *The Pilgrim's Progress* and eighty years after the Restoration. Writing for a bourgeois audience heavily influenced by Puritan domestic theory but removed from the practice of religious martyrdom, Richardson attempts in *Clarissa* to reconstitute the idea of an admirable woman, to make available to women the model of Puritan heroism embodied in Milton's Abdiel, Bunyan's Stand-fast, and the Christ of *Paradise Regained*. Because in a Puritan context any representative trial of female virtue must focus on the heroine's sexual purity, Richardson subjects Clarissa to repeated attempted seductions, culminating in rape, in order to show that a woman's moral character is not contingent upon her physical vulnerability. As Christopher Hill observes, Richardson "puts to the extreme test Milton's proposition" that

> Vertue may be assail'd, but never hurt,
> Surpriz'd by unjust force, but not enthrall'd,
> Yea even that which mischief meant most harm
> Shall in the happy trial prove most glory.
> [C 589–92][1]

1. See Hill, *Puritanism and Revolution*, p. 385.

Richardson, like Milton, explores this proposition through a woman's struggle to stand fast in the face of assaults on her chastity.

Richardson's *Pamela* seems to have been an earlier attempt to show that, even for women, temptation can become the means to virtue. Despite myriad ambushes of her body, Pamela manages to preserve her virginity until marriage, but her earthly success soothes an audience inclined to focus on the material things of this world, on both literal virginity as evidence of spiritual integrity and social recognition as virtue's reward. At the same time, it lays her open to the criticism that her "virtue" was calculated and hypocritical.[2] Richardson emphasizes his own discomfort with this ambiguity in his arguments for *Clarissa*'s tragic ending: "To have a Lovelace for a series of years glory in his wickedness, and think that he had nothing to do, but as an act of grace and favour to hold out his hand to receive that of the best of women, whenever he pleased, and to have it thought, that marriage would be a sufficient amends for all of his enormities to others, as well as to her; [I] could not bear that."[3] Richardson's vehemence in defending the tragic ending of *Clarissa* suggests that he has come to believe, perhaps as a result of such parodies as Fielding's *Shamela* and *Joseph Andrews*, that Pamela's acceptance of Squire B——, even in matrimony, retroactively compromises the virtue of her former refusals. He determines to secure Clarissa against such criticism: "The author of the history (or rather dramatic narrative) of Clarissa, is therefore well justified by the Christian system, in deferring to extricate suffering virtue to the time in which it will meet with the completion of its reward" (4.554). Richardson will not allow any parodic misreading of her story, but he can only prevent that liberty if he defers her happiness until after death, for only in death, in the absolute closure of her story, can Clarissa's perfection be secure.

2. For a survey of contemporary response to *Pamela*, see Ian Donaldson, "Fielding, Richardson, and the Ends of the Novel" *Essays in Criticism* 32 (1982): 26–47.

3. Samuel Richardson, *Clarissa*, 4 vols. (London: J. M. Dent and Sons, 1932), 4:553. All references will be to this edition by volume and page number in the text.

In taking on the issue of female virtue *in terms of* sexual temptation, however, Richardson set for himself an impossible task. He can "prove" Clarissa's sexual virtue in these circumstances only by her persistent refusal to participate in a human sexual relationship. Even marriage to a man other than Lovelace would compromise Richardson's argument about Clarissa's genuine rejection of him because it would allow her refusal to marry Lovelace to be interpreted, by others and by Clarissa herself, as an act of pride; on the other hand, her survival as a single woman would not allow her experience to issue in the triumphal transcendence of human fallibility that constitutes her heroism. Clarissa's perfect goodness fails to dissociate female sexuality from sinfulness because the model on which Richardson constructs her heroism requires the transcendence of body, of what Puritan culture defines as essentially female. Although Clarissa herself manages to achieve heroic stature in her *imitatio Christi* and to take on the role of the Bride of Christ in her triumphal death, her suffering is only personally redemptive. Her triumph comes to involve a renunciation of sexuality itself. Such an defense of female virtue cannot be transferred to good women who do participate in sexual relationships.

For all its romantic-erotic intrigue, *Clarissa* is hardly, as William Beatty Warner would have us believe, a love story "where the right words (and interpretations) at the right instant, could have turned the story of Clarissa and Lovelace from tragedy and death to love and comedy." Richardson's "efforts to make his tragic ending seem necessary" are neither "willful" nor "arbitrary" when read in light of the Puritan tradition of which *Clarissa* is in some sense both a capstone and crystallization. Both Warner's deconstructive reading, which attempts to read *Clarissa* as "several stories, and potential stories, in tension with one another,"[4] and the long line of psychological readings

---

4. William Beatty Warner, "Reading Rape: Marxist-Feminist Configurations of the Literal," *Diacritics* (Winter 1983): 13, 27. Warner's article criticizes both Terry Castle's *Clarissa's Ciphers: Meaning and Disruption in Richardson's "Clarissa"* (Ithaca: Cornell University Press, 1982) and Terry Eagleton's *The Rape of Clarissa: Writing, Sexuality, and Class Struggle* (Minneapolis: University of Minnesota, 1982), two studies critical of his own *Reading Clar-*

privilege, because they are post-Freudian, the eroticism of the unconscious over the intention of the will.[5] In denying the possibility and power of the will or the spirit, they blind themselves to the central issue of the text; their readings, while alert to the nuances of sexual desire and familial politics, cannot acknowledge the validity of Clarissa's moral response to sexual experience.

Christopher Hill suggests that Richardson's "respect for Clarissa's integrity led him to push the Puritan code forward to the point at which its flaw was completely revealed, at which it broke down as a standard of conduct for this world."[6] I would argue that what Richardson's novel chronicles is not the inadequacy of the Puritan code but the failure of the rest of Clarissa's society to live up to it. Clarissa must struggle alone to tailor her behavior to the Christian ideal, to define for herself a model for heroism. Margaret Doody observes that "her life, her vision, and her fate were not envisaged by the friends who gave pious conduct books to young girls in the hope of training dutiful daughters."[7] Clarissa, after one false step occasioned by her great frustration at her family's failure to uphold its side of the bargain of mutual obligations, acts upon her understanding of the Puritan code; Richardson's handling of her trials suggests that the point of that code is not simply to provide an adequate moral standard for this life. Rather, the code sets the stage for the highest form of heroic action and the most perfect happiness possible in it.

---

issa: *The Struggle of Interpretation* (New Haven: Yale University Press, 1979). All three books consider *Clarissa* an illustration of contemporary theories about readers and the nature of writing.

5. In "Karen Horney and *Clarissa*: The Tragedy of Neurotic Pride," *American Journal of Psychoanalysis* 42 (1982): 53, Patricia Reid Elredge regrets that critical discussions approach "pride" as a moral, rather than a psychological, subject. For other readings influenced by contemporary psychological theories, see Cynthia Griffin Wolff, *Samuel Richardson and the Eighteenth-Century Puritan Character* (Hamden, Conn.: Archon, 1972); James Maddox, "Lovelace and the World of Ressentiment in *Clarissa*," *Texas Studies in Literature and Language* 24 (1982): 271–92; and John A. Dussinger, "Love and Consanguinity in Richardson's Novels," *Studies in English Literature* 24 (1984): 513–26.

6. Hill, *Puritanism and Revolution*, p. 388.

7. Margaret Anne Doody, *A Natural Passion: A Study of the Novels of Samuel Richardson* (Oxford: Clarendon Press, 1974), p. 185.

From the beginning of her story, Clarissa and her friends insist on her exemplariness as the cause of her trials.[8] As her friend Anna writes, "Your present trial is but proportioned to your prudence. . . . You see what you draw upon yourself by excelling all your sex" (1.2). Clarissa sets for herself the highest standards she can imagine: absolute, cheerful, and spontaneous obedience to parental authority, the entire negation of individual will. She places herself in the tradition of the Christian daughter and wife as expressed in the Pauline letters, Ecclesiasticus, *Paradise Lost*, and the Puritan domestic treatises.[9] But she also identifies with the Pauline formula that the true Christian life involves *imitatio Christi*, the bearing of persecutions and afflictions in the name of the Gospel. Her model of behavior is a female version of Christ's obedience and sacrifice. In this context, her equation of her father's authority with divine will is exactly appropriate. To conform perfectly to God's will, she must respect and obey his earthly representatives; in obeying her father, she obeys God.[10] By relinquishing to her father control of her grandfather's estate, Clarissa expresses her radical conception of filial duty. When Anna Howe urges her to resume the estate, to wield it as an instrument of power over her obstinate family, Clarissa refuses in terms consistent with her excuses for her mother's passivity: "Is the want of reward, or the want even of a grateful acknowledgement, a reason for us to dispense with what we think our duty?" (1.132). Clarissa's understanding of moral responsibility allows no room for compromise.

In Richardson's world, virtue is a condition that must be continuously re-created, continuously exercised; in both her conflict with her family and her relationship with Lovelace,

8. See John Allen Stevenson, "The Courtship of the Family: Clarissa and the Harlowes Once More," *ELH* 48 (1981): 757–77; and Elredge, "Karen Horney and *Clarissa*," for sensitive analyses—the first Straussian, the other Horneyan—of the Harlowes' family politics.

9. Richardson refers to Ecclesiasticus in *Clarissa*, 4.542. This book from the Apocrypha was recommended to be read from Anglican lecterns each year during the month of October.

10. See Gouge, *Of Domesticall Duties* (London 1622), the fifth treatise; and Jeremy Taylor, *The Rule of Conscience*, in *The Whole Works*, vol. 14, chap. 5, for representative discussions of filial duty.

Clarissa must struggle to maintain her virtue against attack. As Jonathan Loesberg comments: "Not being seduced is not a definitive act."[11] John Allen Stevenson identifies that same impermanence in Clarissa's daughterly virtue: until the conflict over Solmes, he argues, Clarissa's experience of "duty has always coincided with will; she could be 'good,' yet she felt essentially independent."[12] In an early conversation, Clarissa challenges her mother, "I hope, madam, that I have not so behaved hitherto, as to render such a trial of my obedience necessary" (1.78). Charlotte Harlowe, urging her to comply with the Solmes match, poses in return a question that becomes central for the novel and for Clarissa herself. She asks Clarissa "whether you will discredit all your past behaviour" (1.80) by this present disobedience. Mrs. Harlowe poses the question rhetorically; she, of course, believes that disobedience in this "highest instance of duty" *would* undermine all Clarissa's past obedience, would give occasion for others to reinterpret her previous motives. Since the motions of the spirit require careful scrutiny and prudent suspicion, her present uncharacteristic impulse to defiance should cause Clarissa herself to question her motives. But the question is more complex than a simple conflict between parental and personal will. Until this point, Clarissa's duty to her parents has always coincided not merely with her will but also with the dictates of her conscience. Because she cannot marry Solmes and cannot *not* marry him, the only "action" available to her is the refusal to act, which, like not being seduced, is not definitive. Clarissa herself believes that she is obedient but that "deeds are the only evidence of intentions" (1.289). During the course of the novel, Clarissa comes to realize that her standards require of her nothing less than perfection, that, in the exercise of Christian virtue, "obedience without reserve is required of you" (1.224), but that she cannot be obedient and act according to her conscience.

In the insistence of Clarissa's parents that she marry Solmes,

---

11. Jonathan Loesburg, "Allegory and Narrative in *Clarissa*," *Novel* 15 (1981): 52.

12. Stevenson, "Courtship of the Family," 772.

Richardson creates a moral dilemma that promises to truly challenge Clarissa's talents. Her objections to "the odious Solmes" arise not simply from physical disgust; she herself would not consider such an objection adequate to oppose a father's will, although her physical scruples deserve serious respect. Of her father's threat to kneel to obtain her compliance, Clarissa writes, "Yet, had but the sacrifice of *inclination* and *personal preference* been *all*, less than KNEELING would have done. My *duty* should have been the conqueror of my *inclination*" (2.166). Solmes, however, is not simply physically deformed, he is morally stunted. He is willing to disinherit his relations in order to secure Clarissa; he wants to marry her solely for financial aggrandizement. She fears "the marriage intimacies . . . , so *very* intimate," because to give her hand where she cannot give her heart would make her marriage to Solmes a kind of whoredom. Clarissa worries that it would be spiritual suicide as well, because her ideal of spontaneous obedience applies to wives as well as to daughters. She is a woman who thinks "more highly of a *husband's* prerogative than most people do of the *royal* one" (4.45), "who never looked upon any duty, much less a voluntarily-vowed one, with indifference" (2.167), who knows she must obey her husband in all matters not expressly contrary to God's will. Her marriage to the materialist Solmes would compromise her spiritual well-being, "every day, it is likely, rising to witness to some new breach of an altar-vowed duty" (2.287). Her continual insistence that she would rather be bricked up in the family vault than marry Solmes dramatizes the strength of her fear for her spiritual welfare.

Lovelace, however, appears to possess precisely the moral sensibility Solmes lacks: he is generous to his tenants, prudent with his wealth, "no gamester; no horse racer; no fox-hunter; no drinker." He has also impressed Clarissa with conversation she considers "unexceptionable; even chastely so; which, be his actions what they would, showed him capable of being influenced by *decent* company; and that he might probably therefore be a *led* man, rather than a *leader*, in other company" (1.198). Such considerations persuade Clarissa to contemplate "the secret pleasure . . . to be able to reclaim such a man to the paths of virtue and honour: to be a *secondary* means, if I were to be his, of saving him" (1.200). Clarissa's evaluation of Lovelace's character is not as naïve as this discussion might suggest. She takes her cue from Saint Paul: "For the unbelieving husband is sanctified by the wife. . . . For what knowest thou, O wife, whether thou shalt save *thy* husband?" (1 Cor. 7:14, 16). The impulse is charitable and theologically correct; it expresses her desire to perform one of the few kinds of significant work available to women in her day.[13] The reformation scheme is not simply a way to gloss over her attraction to Lovelace. Although she finds him attractive, she would not marry him if such a union should "unsettle me in all my own principles, and hazard my future hopes" (1.201).

Pressed by her family to marry a man she despises, Clarissa struggles to reconcile her duty to her parents with the scruples of her Christian conscience. The compromise Clarissa proposes, that she live single, is not an option in Puritan culture. To propose conditions to her father violates parental authority by asserting an independence already explicitly present and feared in her possession of her grandfather's estate. Moreover, her suggestion that she never marry subverts the social hierarchy by suggesting that a woman is not necessarily sexual and subordinate. Her family's response derives, predictably, from an assumption that female sexual appetite can be governed, that female morality can be assured, only when the woman is the property of some man.[14] James Harlowe expresses the family fear that singleness, like virginity, is an eternally precarious condition: "The liberty of *refusing*, pretty miss, is denied you, because we are all sensible that the liberty of *choosing*, to every one's dislike, must follow" (1.263). The family's response to her offer to live single underscores their contempt for female char-

---

13. Cf. Dorothea's reasons for marrying Casaubon in George Eliot's *Middlemarch*.

14. Christopher Hill offers a discussion of property marriage and life tenancies as the basis for Clarissa's struggles with her family in "Clarissa Harlowe and Her Times." Stevenson, in "Courtship of the Family," offers an alternative Straussian interpretation.

acter and their inability to conceive of the possibility of independent female virtue.

At the height of Clarissa's persecutions, her Aunt Hervey presents the conflict in terms that express her sense of Clarissa's exemplary status: "If you can forbear claiming your estate, and can resolve to avoid Lovelace, you will continue to be the greatest miracle I ever knew at your years" (1.237). But Mrs. Hervey, while hinting that the family may give in to Clarissa's aversion, nevertheless exhorts her, "Conform to your father's will, if you possibly can. How meritorious will it be in you to do so! Pray God to *enable* you to conform. You don't know what may be done" (1.237). The ambiguity of that final comment expresses Clarissa's helplessness. To conform to her own understanding of her filial duty, she must submit passively to her family's desire to sacrifice her to their economic plan. Her only other option—to continue her passive resistance, to await "what may be done"—is simply another form of martyrdom.

If she refused Solmes before her gathered family and in the presence of a clergyman, Clarissa would place herself in the tradition of Christian martyrs for conscience. Although she fears that she might capitulate to the importunities of father and mother, Clarissa asserts, "If consent of heart, and assent of voice, be necessary to a marriage, I am sure I never can, nor ever will be married to Mr. Solmes" (1.404). But unlike Christ, who affirms his faith and obedience even as he expresses his personal fears—"O my Father, if it be possible, let this cup pass from me: nevertheless not as I will, but as thou wilt" (Matt. 26:39)—Clarissa abandons passive resistance for active disobedience. She runs away from the trial.[15]

Running away forces Clarissa to reevaluate both her own character and her conception of Christian duty. Her first letter to Anna after she has run off with Lovelace expresses her attempt to come to terms with a vision of herself as a person who could do such "a rash and inexcusable thing" (1.471). Once, she

<hr/>

15. While Wolff discusses many of the issues with which I am concerned in this chapter, her application of modern psychological perspective to the Puritan experience hinders her ability to appreciate either Clarissa's heroism or her theology.

had been able to argue that "we have nothing to do but to choose what is right; to be steady in pursuit of it; and to leave the issue to Providence" (1.94). Now, she has failed her own conception of her self on two counts: rather than trusting to Providence, she has acted, and in acting, she has sanctioned her family's misinterpretation of her intentions. Before her flight, she could write with aggrieved integrity, "What I call *steadiness* is deemed stubbornness, obstinacy, prepossession, by those who have a right to put what interpretation they please upon my conduct" (1.94). Now she can no longer trust the purity of her intentions; she has behaved in a very "unsteady" manner. She must face up to her own belief that "*deeds* are to me the only evidences of *intentions*" (1.289).

Because he holds her to the extraordinary standards of Christian heroism, Richardson will not allow Clarissa's suffering to become an excuse for her failure to face her trial. Clarissa's situation at home had become intolerable; her brother and sister turned the family against her for selfish and vengeful reasons; she was, of course, partially tricked away. But Clarissa cannot excuse herself because of others' follies: she believes with Mrs. Howe that "a prudent daughter will not wilfully err, because her parents err, if they *were* to err: if she *do*, the world which blames the parents, will not acquit the child" (1.298). Once out of her father's house, she can no longer console herself "that I have not, by my own inadvertence or folly, brought myself into this sad situation" (1.418). She must question her past motives and judge them against her own standard of conduct. Margaret Doody argues that "the novel depends on her departure being a conscious act, and, to some extent, a choice, although a choice made by Clarissa in a moment of great agitation."[16] Like Milton's Eve, she has, through an action "out of her nature," created the moral as well as literal occasion for her new trial. In corresponding with Lovelace and granting him a clandestine interview, Clarissa has opened a potentially disas-

---

16. Doody, *A Natural Passion*, p. 137. See also Janet Butler, "The Garden: Early Symbol of Clarissa's Complicity," *Studies in English Literature* 24 (1984): 527–44.

trous gap in her obedience. The rest of the novel chronicles her struggle to repair her error.

II

Once Lovelace's letters begin to dominate the novel, the terms of Clarissa's trial seem to change. *Clarissa* shifts from being a story of family conflict to being a tale of attempted seduction. But filial obedience and sexual purity actually express mirror aspects of the Puritan conception of female virtue. Both require the negation of self, the radical subordination of individual will or desire. Although Lovelace asks not "Is she obedient" but "If she be really angel or woman[?]" (2.140), he too questions the continuity between her speech and her inner emotions, between her intentions and her deeds. Like Clarissa's family, he asks, "Has her virtue ever been *proved*?" (2.36). Most important, he poses the question Clarissa has been asking herself, which Richardson knows his readers will ask: "Is then the divine Clarissa capable of *loving* a man she ought *not* to love? And is she capable of *affectation*? And is her virtue founded in *pride*? And if the answers to these questions be affirmative, must she not then be a *woman*?" (2.38). These questions echo her brother's and uncle's sneers about her modesty and her stated aversion to Solmes; they are questions warranted by her secret correspondence and flight.

Lovelace can conceive of only two kinds of women: those who are easily seduced and those who resist for the wrong reasons. He rejects the possibility of a sexually chaste woman, of a woman who feels desires yet refrains from acting upon them in what she considers to be an immoral context. Having no self-discipline himself, he cannot imagine such a quality in anyone else. He has found Clarissa among her friends a formidable adversary, but her unpremeditated flight suggests to him that she may be vulnerable: she allowed fear to overpower reason. He playfully asks Belford if he might have permission "to try if I cannot awaken the *woman* in her? To try if she . . . be really inflexible as to the grand article?" (2.42). His scheme creates for Richardson the conditions under which Clarissa's love of virtue "for its own sake" can be "proved." Once she is isolated and completely dependent upon Lovelace, her reputation ruined, the true motive of her chastity—love of virtue—will become indisputable.

As Lovelace defines it, however, the trial will determine not whether Clarissa is virtuous but whether she is "human." He understands virtue and vice in terms of angelic frigidity and animal sexuality. If he can "awaken the *woman* in her" (2.38), he will have proven her fallen. The terms of his test make no distinction between licit and illicit sexual passion. He cannot conceive of innocent sexuality: desire equals sinfulness. When Clarissa expresses her modesty, Lovelace calls it "an angelic delicacy which sets you above all our sex, and even above your own" (2.90). In a letter to Belford, Lovelace comments of Miss Howe: "She has a high opinion of her sex, to think they can charm so long a man so well acquainted with their *identicalness*" (2.370). He hopes in his siege of Clarissa to reduce her to this common female identicalness; he wants to prove that she is simply woman, simply body, simply vagina. But such an identity would do more than force Clarissa to recognize her sexuality. It would lead, as the rape threatens to do, to her classing herself with "the vilest of her sex" (3.237). Clarissa understands the difference between sanctified and sinful sex. If she were to surrender to her attraction to Lovelace, she would have to accept not sexuality but her sinful self.[17]

Clarissa's story is tragic not because of her own rigidity but because of her society's failure to evaluate women as anything but sexual beings. The novel supposes that Clarissa, had she been presented with a spiritually acceptable alternative to both Lovelace and Solmes, could have participated in human sex-

---

17. On this point, I differ from the otherwise insightful studies of *Clarissa* and Puritanism by Ian Watt, *The Rise of the Novel: Studies in Defoe, Richardson, and Fielding* (Berkeley: University of California Press, 1957); and Mary Poovey, "Journeys from This World to the Next: The Providential Promise in *Clarissa* and *Tom Jones*," *ELH* 43 (1976): 300–15. Puritans distinguish between rejecting the flesh, which involves rejecting God's creation, and rejecting the sinful self.

uality in a positive way. Her suggestion that she live single seems at first a response to her frustration over the suitors her family proposes, then a compromise she hopes will resolve her conflict with her family while repairing her reputation in the eyes of the world, and finally the only logical option for a person who has suffered so much in this world that she has been thoroughly weaned from it. Her rejection of marriage and human happiness is a position forced upon her by the misogyny of those around her, both in her own family and in Lovelace's sinful community.

Convinced of her folly in fleeing with Lovelace, Clarissa repents her correspondence and blames her "presumption" in thinking she could "be the arbitress of the quarrels of unruly spirits" (1.486). She writes to Anna that she is "punished, as I frequently think, for my vanity in hoping to be an *example* to young persons of my sex!" (2.73). Her statement indicates not only her understanding of her own psychology but her belief in God's active intervention in human history. She interprets all her misfortunes and suffering, from her imprisonment at home to her night at the sponging house, as correctives to her overconfidence in her own virtuous sufficiency. Suspicious even of her charity and piety, she wonders, "Is not vanity, or secret love of praise, a principal motive with me at bottom? Ought I not to suspect my own heart?" (1.92). Her continual self-criticism suggests that her predicament, like that of Milton's Eve, derives from a sense of self-sufficiency, which, when expressed in the female, initiates disaster. She erred in imagining that she could control her family or Lovelace, but above all, she erred in imagining that she could perfectly control herself.

Richardson's religious convictions allow Clarissa a chance to repent her flight, which indicated her lack of faith in God's saving intervention, a chance to recognize her folly in trusting to her own vigilance and strength. Her genuine and fully conscious repentance of her disobedience will negate her unwitting error. Recognizing that her attraction to Lovelace was stronger than she knew, Clarissa determines to discipline herself to know and to act upon her own intentions, rather than her affections. Earlier, when Anna Howe teased her about her attachment, she protested, "Indeed I would not be *in love* with him, as it is called, for the world" (1.47). Now, shocked into recognizing the power of her own physical desire, she laments, "Let this evermore be my caution to individuals of my sex: Guard your eyes: 'twill ever be in combination against your judgment" (2.277).

But although her eyes seduced her into beginning the fatal correspondence with Lovelace, closer observation corrects her perspective. Her rejection of concupiscence of the eyes follows immediately upon her awareness of it. She now considers marriage to him only as a sorry compromise in an already blighted life. As she admonishes Anna, "But you must not, my dear, suppose my heart to be still a confederate with my eye. That deluded eye now clearly sees its fault, and the misled heart despises it for it" (2.277). She must discipline her eyes and heart so that her initial "false step" does not lead her inevitably to destruction.

Although her family's obstinacy and her inability to find shelter among friends force Clarissa to return reluctantly to her original plan of reforming Lovelace through marriage, his continual teasings and threats reinforce her repentance and her watchfulness. Lovelace encourages her desire to reform him, playing up to what he hopes is a weak point in her defenses, as Satan plays to Sin's needs in *Paradise Lost*, Book 2, and later tailors his seduction to Eve's particular weaknesses. Lovelace proposes to reform through Clarissa's example, appealing to her pride in her virtue and influence. He asks her advice about the import of past "good motions" and claims that she was sent to save his soul (2.60, 72). But Lovelace is not prepared for Clarissa's ardent watchfulness. Confronted by her reserve, he decides: "I must, therefore, make my first effort by surprise. There may possibly be some *cruelty* necessary: but there may be *consent in struggle*; there may be *yielding in resistance*" (2.245). He hopes for "a yielding reluctance" (2.495), arguing that "there is no triumph in *force*. No conquest over the will" (2.398). Yet Lovelace would resort willingly to rape if he could be sure that it would reduce Clarissa to that complete dependence on his pleasure that her public disgrace, isolation, and confinement have failed to achieve. The "seduction" he plans will be calculated and nonsexual: his pride, not his desire, requires her consent.[18]

Clarissa's watchfulness signals her role as Puritan heroine. Aware of her own vulnerability, she adopts a strategy of constant alertness modeled on the parable of the wise and foolish virgins and the New Testament injunction: "Watch ye therefore, and pray always, that ye may be accounted worthy to escape all these things that shall come to pass, and to stand before the Son of man" (Luke 21:36). Clarissa suspects Lovelace's protestations to reform, which carefully avoid appealing to divine grace, and rightly fears for her safety. She will not accept any bed partners; she refuses to undress until her maid has left her for the night. She explains to Anna that "I ought to apprehend everything" and, should she find her suspicions justified, "fly the house and the man as I would an infection" (2.232). When Lovelace does gain entrance to her chamber, pretending to be terrified for her safety because of a fire he has had set,[19] she resists his embraces by sliding to the floor and threatening to stab herself with a pair of scissors. After discovering the kind of house in which Lovelace has placed Clarissa and the complexity of the snares he has woven around her, Anna exclaims, "But if this be so, what [it would be asked by an indifferent person] has hitherto saved you? Glorious creature! What, morally speaking, but your watchfulness! What but that, and the majesty of your virtue" (3.9). Lovelace himself is forced to remark after her death that "a *meek and gentle temper* was hers, though a *true heroine*, whenever honour or virtue called for an exertion of spirit" (4.523).

Clarissa's majestic virtue frequently stuns her tormentors. She shares with Spenser's Una and Belphoebe and Milton's Lady from *Comus* an aura of Minervan invulnerability and influence. Lovelace attributes his impulsive marriage proposals to this effect (see 2.142); he writes to Belford that her presence

18. See Loesberg, "Allegory and Narrative," pp. 47–48.

19. Wolff mistakenly supposes that Lovelace had not ordered the fire set; her misreading forces her to accuse Clarissa of a desire to be seduced, which she expresses unconsciously in her fear of rape.

"stuns" and "awes" him, that she "half-assimilates me to her own virtue" (2.400). But as with Milton's Eve, Clarissa's virtuous presence does not afford her complete protection. Just as Satan's admiration quickly sours to jealousy and hatred, Lovelace's awe of Clarissa angers him; he writes to Belford that she "urge[s] her destiny" by defying him (2.31). Indeed, her virtue seems to incite others not necessarily to virtue but to a powerful expression of their own true character. Clarissa's goodness inspires admiration and charity in Anna, Belford, and the Smiths, who shelter her after she escapes from the brothel, but it goads Bella, James, and the women at Mrs. Sinclair's to greater viciousness.

Like Satan in *Paradise Lost*, Lovelace resists in himself the "good motions" Clarissa inspires, as he resists Belford's entreaties. Of one encounter, he writes, "I went into my chamber, and locked myself in; ashamed of being awed by her majestic loveliness, and apprehensive virtue" (2.377). His stunned admiration lasts, however, only as long as he is in her presence. He records his fear that "this sweet creature will at last undo me!" (2.389) but hardens his heart against her influence. In a telling passage, Lovelace describes a "strange emotion" to Belford and then scientifically analyzes it as "something choking, as it were, in my throat—I know not how—yet, I must needs say, though I am out of countenance upon the recollection, that there was something very pretty in it; and I wish I could know it again, that I might have a more perfect idea of it, and be better able to *describe it* to thee" (2.461–62, italics mine). This repeated pattern of examining and then rejecting moments of feeling places Lovelace securely in the camp of the damned.[20] He refuses to listen to Clarissa, Belford, or the motions of his own heart; symbolically murders his conscience in a long, playful letter; purposely misinterprets his dream of Clarissa's ascension; and after her death, rejects any feelings of remorse as "fruitless reflections" (4.440). The tension between his good

20. See Gillian Beer, "Richardson, Milton, and the Status of Evil," *Review of English Studies* 19 (1968): 261–70, for an extended discussion of the literary relationship between Lovelace and the Satan of *Paradise Lost*. Beer's essay also anticipates my discussion of Clarissa's similarity to the Lady in *Comus*.

impulses and his reckless will to evil elevates him to the status of a worthy adversary for Clarissa and contributes to the moral seriousness of the tragedy.

III

One month after the rape, Anna describes Clarissa's situation in terms of a journey: "Like a traveller who has been put out of his way by the overflowing of some rapid stream, you have only had the foreright path you were in overwelmed. A few miles about, a day or two only lost, as I may say, and you are in a way to recover it; and, by your quickening speed, will get up the lost time" (3.416). She encourages Clarissa to "improve upon the allegory, as you know how," advising her to marry Lovelace. But while Anna's allegory affords a telling insight into the nature of Clarissa's predicament, her interpretation of it misconstrues the nature of the "path" Clarissa was in. Clarissa originally thought, like Anna, that her one false step—leaving her father's house—committed her and Lovelace to "one plain path" (2.377) leading to an honorable and paternally authorized marriage. Lovelace, however, understood from the beginning the seriousness of that one false step. He imagines before them not Clarissa's plain path but a pleasant ramble, remarking to Belford, "As I have picked up the sweet traveller in my way, I cannot help wishing that she would bear me company in the *rest* of my journey, although she were to step out of her own path to oblige me" (3.178). Richardson has Lovelace use this metaphor of the journey to stress Clarissa's folly in placing herself in his power. He comments of her unwitting "choosing" to lodge at Mrs. Sinclair's brothel, "Silly little rogues! to walk out into by-paths on the strengths of their own judgments!" (2.113). Her false step has led her out of her "way"; as *The Pilgrim's Progress* documents, getting back in is a difficult business.

But Richardson allows Clarissa not only time to repent her disobedient flight but a second trial. Like Milton's Eve, she has created the occasion for temptation through overvaluing herself. But just as Eve departed from Adam's side "still sinless" and remained so until she actually ate of the fruit, Clarissa's false step need not prove fatal. If she can resist the temptations and pressures of her earthly situation—the pressure to "make the best of it" by marrying Lovelace against her principles—and can remain faithful to her conception of Christian duty, she can recover her path. Richardson offers her the rape as both a second chance and the most definitive trial.

Both Clarissa and Richardson view the rape not as evidence of secret sexual desire but as punishment for her overconfidence in her own judgment, in the sufficiency of her own virtue. During her drugged hysteria following the rape, she writes, "I have been a very wicked creature—a vain, proud, poor creature—full of secret pride—which I carried off under an humble guise, and deceived everybody—my sister says so—and now I am punished" (3.212). While her mental disorder causes her to blame herself for the rape, the discarded scraps of paper which Dorcas collects from the floor harp on pride, not lust. She tells herself that she is "humbled in the dust" because of her "vanity" and "self-assurance" (3.206). She remembers and assents to Bella's accusation that her "proud heart" hid behind only a "thin veil of humility" (3.206). The rape forces her to radically reconsider her past behavior and motives. She condemns her pride in her own virtue: "I thought I could acquit my intention of any such vanity. I was too secure in the knowledge I thought I had of my own heart. My supposed advantage became a snare to me. And what now is the end of all?" (3.207). But Clarissa's situation is not so desperate as she imagines, if only she can persevere in her refusal of Lovelace.

After the rape, Clarissa rejects Lovelace in terms that express her conception of marriage as a sacred covenant: "It would be *criminal* in me to wish to bind my soul in *covenant* to a man so nearly allied to perdition" (3.223). Such a union would place her in a hypocritical and morally suspect position. Lady Sarah's praise expresses the importance of her refusal in maintaining her reputation: "Her virtue is not the least questionable. She could not resent as she does, had she anything to reproach herself with" (3.303). Clarissa agrees, confiding to Anna, "I should not think my penitence for the rash step I took, anything better than a specious delusion, if I had not got above the least wish to have Mr. Lovelace for my husband" (3.519). Clarissa cannot marry Lovelace because she recognizes that her acceptance of him would retroactively reinterpret the rape as a seduction, as Squire B——'s proposal of marriage to Pamela and her acceptance mitigates the perceived threat of his earlier assaults. Lovelace's idea that marriage transforms injuries to Clarissa into kindnesses to Mrs. Lovelace reinforces this perception. But far more serious, cohabitation with Lovelace, even in marriage, would excuse his past behavior, compromise her moral integrity, and be in a real sense "living in sin."

While Clarissa believes that a true marriage sacrament sanctifies, her vows to the unrepentant Lovelace would destroy her. Her vivid early dream of Lovelace trying to bury her in a grave full of decomposing corpses has proven prophetic. The premeditation and brutality of the rape fixes Lovelace's godlessness clearly in her mind. Saint Paul encourages believers to keep their nonbelieving partners, affirming that the believing spouse may save the other. But he also charges single Christians to marry within the faith, rather than knowingly to unite themselves with the sinful: "Be ye not unequally yoked together with unbelievers: for what fellowship hath righteousness with unrighteousness? and what communion hath light with darkness?" (2 Cor. 6:14). Clarissa challenges Anna, "Can I vow duty to one so wicked, and hazard my salvation by joining myself to so great a profligate, now I *know* him to be so?" (3.519). Once she has identified Lovelace's depravity, Clarissa rejects him clearly and decisively; although the rape has shattered her self-confidence, it has not impinged on her spiritual integrity.

The novel insists that the rape did not violate Clarissa's will. Lovelace himself absolves her of any complicity, assuring Belford that she was not "subdued by *her own* consent, or any the *least* yielding in her will" (3.202). He declares that drugging her had been an unavoidable stratagem, because "all the princes of the air, or beneath it, joining with me, could never have subdued her while she had her senses" (3.218). His decision to continue the "trial" with a second attempt designed to determine "whether she cannot be brought to make the best of an irreparable evil" (3.200) reveals his sense that he has not accomplished his desire; when she escapes his control, he is reduced to hoping that pregnancy will force her to marry him to legitimate the child (4.38). Mrs. Norton and Anna both write to comfort Clarissa "in the triumphs of a virtue unsullied; a will wholly faultless" (3.384); Clarissa herself can come to understand, as Christiana cannot, that rape does not in and of itself threaten her salvation—"I presume to hope that I have a mind that cannot be debased, in *essential instances*, by temporal calamities" (3.503)—but she cannot say this of her body. She believes it has been defiled, that she can only be purified by leaving it.

Unlike Bunyan, who conflates a woman's spiritual and physical state, Richardson allows his heroine to transcend her body, or sinful self. Early in his attempt on Clarissa's virtue, Lovelace asks defiantly, "Can a girl be *degraded by trials*, who is not *overcome?*" (1.327). The answer, for Clarissa, is clearly *yes*. She considers herself physically defiled and degraded, referring to herself as "a creature whom thou hast levelled with the dirt of the street, and classed with the vilest of her sex" (3.237). But her purification, unlike Christiana's literal bath, is a spiritual cleansing. Mrs. Norton identifies Clarissa's sufferings as redemptive, for "if you have your purification in [this life], you will be the more happy" (3.330). She assures Clarissa, "You are therefore in the direct road to glory, however thorny the path you are in" (4.108–9).

Clarissa learns to view her life, as Mrs. Norton encourages her, as "a state of probation" (3.330) and purification, writing to Anna, "And who knows but that this very path into which my inconsideration has thrown me, strewed as it is with briers and thorns which tear in pieces my gaudier trappings, may not be the right path to lead me into the great road to my future happiness" (3.18). Eve ultimately leaves Eden to accompany Adam down an uncertain path; Christiana journeys after her husband along a hazardous road. Like Christiana, Clarissa encounters the hazards of the way, but she, too, manages to regain the proper path. Anna errs in imagining that for Clarissa to recover "the overwhelmed path for the sake of future passengers who travel the same way" (3.416), she should marry Lovelace. Clarissa's path leads toward union, but not on earth. She looks forward to the fellowship of the saints in heaven: her journey, like Christiana's, moves toward completion in fellowship and backward to Eden. She, too, hears and obeys her Lord's command "Follow me."

Richardson dwells on Clarissa's journey toward death because her death secures her status as Puritan heroine. The novel could not guarantee her continued purity should she survive beyond its close, and marriage to someone other than Lovelace would suggest that she does not truly prefer the life of the spirit, or "a single state," as she now claims. Her trial and suffering have weaned her affections from this world; the path she is in leads, like that of Bunyan's Faithful, inevitably toward a martyr's death. Before the rape, Clarissa wrote to Anna, "If I could flatter myself that my indifference to all the joys of this life proceeded from *proper* motives, and not rather from the disappointments and mortifications my pride has met with, how much rather, I think, should I choose to be wedded to my shroud than to any man on earth" (2.176). After the rape, confident that her pride has been broken, she can detach herself from this world for the right reasons.

Clarissa expresses her weaning from the world in terms of sexual as well as physical denial, partly because sexual desire is the salient metaphor in Puritan culture for the attractions of this world, a world personified by such figures as Bunyan's Wanton and Madam Bubble. But Clarissa, believing that her complacent willingness to die "becomes a person who has had such a weaning-time as I have been favoured with" (4.216), places the purpose of her weaning in explicitly sexual terms. Her God is a jealous God, who *"will have no rivals in the hearts of those He sanctifies"* (4.302). She assures Mrs. Norton that "I am upon a *better preparation* than for an earthly husband" (4.2). She refers to her entire burial preparation, especially her choice of clothes, in terms of a wedding, exulting, "Never bride was so ready as I am. My wedding garments are bought. . . . yet will they be the easiest, the *happiest* suit, that ever bridal maiden wore" (4.303). But while sexual repression becomes almost a metonomy for "weaned affections," other ties to the world require breaking. Belford records Clarissa's claim that the revocation of her father's curse "and a last blessing, are all I have to wish for" (3.507); although her father recalls the curse, the last blessing and all other forms of earthly consolation are denied her.

Richardson has Clarissa recover for women the possibility of a mystical-erotic relationship with God. She prepares not simply to die but to greet her Bridegroom, Christ, in heaven; the injunction, "a man shall leave his father and mother, and shall cleave unto his wife, and they shall be one flesh" (Gen. 2:24), applies to heavenly marriages as well. As she exclaims on her deathbed, "GOD ALMIGHTY WOULD NOT LET ME DEPEND FOR COMFORT UPON ANY BUT HIMSELF" (4.339). Belford's description of her dying words expresses the breathlessness of a death that is also an ecstasy: "And now—and now [holding up her almost lifeless hands for the last time]—come— O come—blessed Lord—JESUS!" (4.347). Although Richardson's description of Clarissa's death stops short of the supernatural, Lovelace's proleptic dream offers in baroque splendor the omitted account of Clarissa's triumphant ascension: "The most angelic form I had ever beheld, all clad in transparent white, descended in a cloud, which, opening, discovered a firmament above it, crowded with golden cherubs and glittering seraphs, all addressing her with: Welcome, welcome, welcome! and, encircling my charmer, ascended with her to the region of seraphims" (4.136).

IV

Richardson writes in the Preface to *Clarissa* that Clarissa's validity as "an exemplar to her sex" depends upon her humanity. He defends her faults as necessary to her heroic stature: "To have been impeccable, must have left nothing for the divine grace and a purified state to do, and carried our idea of her from woman to angel" (xiv). This transubstantiation is, however, precisely what seems to happen in the course of the novel. Clarissa exhibits the strength of her commitment to virtue; she rises above human emotion and frailty, declaring to Anna that if love is allowed to excuse "our most unreasonable follies, and to lay level all the fences that a careful education has surrounded us by, what is meant by the doctrine of subduing our passions?" (2.438). Her trials purify her will and wean her affections from the world. *Clarissa* becomes, then, a *Paradise Lost* in which Eve resists temptation, or, more precisely, a female version of *Paradise Regained*. Clarissa learns to say, "in humble imitation of the sublimest Exemplar. . . , Lord, it is Thy will; and it shall be mine. Thou art just in all thy dealings with the children of men; and I know Thou wilt not afflict me beyond what I can bear: and if I *can* bear it, I *ought* to bear it; and (Thy grace assisting me), I *will* bear it" (3.522). Clarissa, like the Christ whom she imitates, proves herself "sufficient to stand," but in her sufficiency she transcends her sex. Because her heroism depends on the wholesale rejection of sexuality, Clarissa's holy death does not redeem the reputation of other women. Rather, her success simply highlights the failure of the rest of her sex to live up to her example.

Despite Richardson's desire to offer a model of female virtue, Clarissa's heroism is so exemplary that it becomes inimitable. It requires complete self-negation and a martyr's death. As the bride of Christ, Clarissa perfectly expresses the model of female subordination and obedience that, in her mother's passivity, gave rise to her own tragic situation. Just as the terms of Clarissa's trial were constructed to prove not her virtuous womanhood but her asexuality, the terms of her victory are wholly negative. Although Clarissa's fall, had it been effected, would have damned "the whole of her sex," her victory is nontransferable. Anna comments that a portrait of Clarissa's character would be "surrounded with such a flood of brightness, with such a glory, that it would indeed dazzle; but leave one heartless to imitate" (2.131). Anna's compromise in marrying her dull suitor Hickman indicates her own discouragement. Clarissa becomes increasingly "other," placing herself apart from other women, as Lovelace does in declaring her an angel. She writes to Anna, "Let me repeat that I am quite sick of life; and of an earth in which *innocent* and *benevolent* spirits are sure to be considered as *aliens,* and to be made sufferers by the *genuine sons* and *daughters* of *that earth"* (4.383). Her declaration establishes that, while the suffering she has been subjected to has been "inhuman," her persecutors are only too human.

Richardson, far from presenting Clarissa's plight as a representative instance of sexual politics, seems to be as concerned to define rape as only the most extreme and unusual instance of violence as to prove that Clarissa is virtuous. He has Lovelace affirm society's perception of rape as less than a crime by declaring that "whatever rapes have been attempted, none ever were committed, one person to one person" without "a yielding reluctance" (2.495). Lovelace assures Joseph Leman that "rapes are unnatural things; and more *rare* than are imagined" (2.148), and though Lovelace may not seem to be the most reliable authority on this subject, Belford, reformed and sobered, agrees. Richardson summarizes one of Belford's letters: "He distinguishes, however, between an irreparable injury intended to a CLARISSA, and one designed to *such* of the sex as contribute by their weakness and indiscretion to their own fall, and thereby entitle themselves to a large share of the guilt" (4.458). Richardson enlists the aid of his plot to insure that Clarissa's rape is in fact "rape": he makes sure that she is unknowingly drugged and provides his villain with an army of accomplices. Indeed, under the terms Richardson has set up, it would appear that the rape of Clarissa is the only one ever to have deserved such a title. Most victims, it seems, are still guilty of having been victimized; physical weakness, which is in these terms indistinguishable from moral weakness, is a crime deserving punishment.

But the common woman is not simply a helpless and pathetic victim in *Clarissa;* Mrs. Sinclair and her whores come to be identified as the inciters and orchestrators of Clarissa's trials. Although Lovelace has seduced and ruined many of the women in the brothel, it is only at their instigation that he commits the one rape Richardson and Belford are so careful to distinguish from all other apparent acts of rape. Belford certainly fears the whores as a bad influence, begging Lovelace, "let not the specious devils thou hast brought her among be suffered to triumph over her; nor make her the victim of *unmanly artifices*" (2.254); Lovelace himself expresses anxiety over their ridiculing his virility and courage. Writing to Belford, Lovelace argues: "A fallen woman is a worse devil than even a profligate man. The former is incapable of remorse: that am not I—nor ever shall *they prevail upon me*, though aided by all the powers of darkness, to treat this amiable creature with indignity" (2.208, italics mine). With the politics of the situation so defined, Lovelace, when he commits the rape, becomes yet another victim of Mrs. Sinclair and her house. While this presentation of himself as helpless victim is in part posturing on Lovelace's part, it pervades the novel powerfully enough to have led one critic to suggest that Lovelace could not have committed the rape himself, that Mrs. Sinclair's women carried out Clarissa's defloration with a blunt instrument.[21] Even after the rape, Lovelace seems curiously dependent on the women, declaring that if Clarissa will not marry him, he will "give an uninterrupted hearing, not to my conscience, but to these women below" (3.278). Just as Anna fulfils the role of an external conscience for Clarissa to test herself against, the whores at Mrs. Sinclair's become Lovelace's devils, inciting him to further acts of violence and evil.

In *The Rape of Clarissa*, Terry Eagleton points out that Richardson "can ensure the victory of Clarissa only by fetishizing her, as Lovelace does," that "woman as Madonna is the only response to woman as whore."[22] Eagleton attributes to the novel a positive vision of female possibility. But Richardson

21. See Judith Wilt, "He Could Go No Farther: A Modest Proposal about Lovelace and Clarissa," *PMLA* 92 (1977): 19–32. Wilt's proposal that "Lovelace did not rape Clarissa; that the rape either was not fully carried out or was carried out by the man's female 'accomplices'" (p. 19), fails to account for Lovelace's increased frustration that Clarissa seems no more humbled after the rape than before; Wilt's portrayal of Lovelace as an impotent victim, who was himself "raped" as a youth (p. 22), seriously belies the reading experience of both those who admire Lovelace's daring and jouissance and those who consider him the basest of villains. Her essay does, however, offer a powerful reading of how the women at Mrs. Sinclair's house, and indeed woman as a species, become the novel's repository for human evil and its locus for disgust at the sexual body.

22. Eagleton, *Rape of Clarissa*, p. 86.

does not offer a conventionally understood madonna as his antidote to Lovelace's depraved view of women; he counters with an espoused virgin, a Bride of Christ. Richardson's praise of woman conspicuously prevents the celebration of wholesome sexuality and lawful generation. Sexuality and infection appear inseparably in the text. In an early letter to Clarissa, Colonel Morden warns her that traveled men have "foreign diseases" (2.259). Belford, after his visit to Mrs. Sinclair's sick chamber, declares, with loathing, that the women in their morning dishabille remind him of "Swift's Yahoos, or Virgil's obscene harpies, squirting their ordure upon the Trojan trenchers" (4.381). Comparing them to Clarissa, he declares "that as a neat and clean woman must be an angel of a creature, so a sluttish one is the impurest animal in nature" (4.381). For Richardson, as for his Puritan predecessors, the infection of sinfulness remains located in the sexual female body. Richardson allows Belford to renounce his promiscuous past, and his reformation leads toward marriage with a respectable woman. But Richardson denies any of his whores the opportunity of reformation: Lovelace's well-born conquests die, inevitably, in childbirth; Sally Martin dies of a fever and Polly Horton of a cold. Belford includes in his summary of their histories a quote from Ecclesiasticus that Lovelace applied to Sally: *"There is no wickedness like the wickedness of a woman"* (4.542).

Before he dies, Lovelace curses Mrs. Sinclair, declaring to Belford that "all, all, but what is owing to [Clarissa's] relations, is the fault of that woman, and of her hell-born nymphs" (4.441). That Lovelace ends up blaming the women for his mistreatment of Clarissa may simply show his inability to confront his responsibility and guilt. But Mrs. Sinclair, too, even though she dies in a terrible agony, unrepentant and unregenerate, places all the blame on herself and her women: "For though it was that wicked man's fault that ever she was in my house, yet it was mine, and yours, and yours, and yours, devils as we all were . . . , that he did not do her justice!" (4.383). Like Madam Bubble in Part 2 of *The Pilgrim's Progress*, the evil women become scapegoats, bearing the sins of all the men who frequent their brothel. Clarissa, in her *imitatio Christi*, also becomes a scapegoat, for as Lovelace declares of her, "All thy family's sins are upon thy head" (1.515). That one set of scapegoats is evil and one scapegoat is innocent makes no difference in terms of their experience of earthly suffering, an earthly suffering mandated, according to Puritan theology, by biological necessity.

5

Adultery versus Idolatry: The Hierarchy of Sin in *The Scarlet Letter*

I

Looking back at the Puritan world from the middle nineteenth century, Nathaniel Hawthorne attempts to locate *The Scarlet Letter* in a reconstructed Puritan milieu without privileging its perspective.[1] He tries simultaneously to present the complexities and expose the fallacies of the Puritan allegorical world view. In the sketch "Mrs. Hutchinson," Michael Colacurcio notes, as part of "the moral argument against Calvinism," Hawthorne shows how seventeenth-century theological metaphors enabled Ann Hutchinson's contemporaries to reduce the antinomian crisis to a sexual one. As a protodeconstructionist, Hawthorne reads the metaphysical implications of

1. Lawrence Buell's "Rival Romantic Interpretations of New England Puritanism: Hawthorne versus Stowe," *Texas Studies in Literature and Language* 25 (1983): 77–99, argues that "Hawthorne's fictional treatments of Puritanism are apt to be as much about the problem and process of reconstructing the Puritan era as a dramatization of it" (82); he identifies in Hawthorne's writings about New England Puritanism the detachment of an intellectual historian who "continued to see it as a seventeenth-century phenomenon" (84). Buell adds, however, that "his figurative strategies are likely to have been equally if not more informed by non–New England sources like Spenser's *Faerie Queene* and Bunyan's *Pilgrim's Progress*" (93). Hawthorne's interest in Puritanism is not purely nationalist nor his understanding of it provincial.

the Puritan discussion surrounding Hutchinson literally, in "a clear recognition of the antisocial meaning of self-conscious female sexuality, first formulated in the theological context of Puritan heresy."[2] In *The Scarlet Letter*, however, the clarity of that critical vision falters. Hawthorne attempts to undermine the Puritan community's judgment of Hester by employing a sentimental nineteenth-century narrator, uninformed about the spiritual complexities of the story he tells. But Hawthorne cannot adequately distance himself from the Puritan perspective on Hester's affair because the transcendentalist alienation of self from world, including body, simply restates the Puritan problem with sexuality in other terms.

The Puritan problem is, simply, the tension between love of this world and devotion to God, and its salient locus is the female sexual body. In Puritan literature, a man, as Spenser's Guyon and Bunyan's Stand-fast illustrate, can transcend biological reality: he can resist and deny the impulses of the flesh embodied in the sexuality of "fallen women." Women, spiritually defined by their biological capability—as wife, mother, adulteress, whore—remain trapped in their physical bodies. Because Hawthorne recognizes that Puritanism superimposes spiritual meaning onto physical and biological reality, he tries, in Hester's adultery and in Pearl's humanity, to reduce "the Puritan problem" to the human and literal level, to a repression of sexual passion. Hawthorne explores the "significance" of human sexuality through adultery because the adulterous act, with its visible consequences, allows private passion to become a public topic, to become the subject of a novel.

But the action chronicled in the romance itself is idolatry, not adultery. The sin that intrigues Hawthorne in *The Scarlet Letter* is not the offstage sin of passion but Chillingworth's attempts to seduce Dimmesdale to despair. *The Scarlet Letter* reaffirms a hierarchy of sin which elevates the crime of the spirit over the crime of the flesh by appropriating sexuality as a metaphor for spiritual truth. Hester's adultery, instead of being a literaliza-

---

2. Michael Colacurcio, "Footsteps of Ann Hutchinson," *English Literary History* 39 (1972): 472.

tion of the Puritan discomfort with the physical world, becomes an earthly shadow of a greater spiritual sin. Dimmesdale, the bride of Christ whose spiritual chastity is threatened, becomes the heroine of *The Scarlet Letter*. In making him such, Hawthorne reenacts the artistic displacement of the female present in Puritan allegorical texts: Stand-fast represents chastity better than Christiana; Christ expresses female subordination and obedience more perfectly than Eve. Dimmesdale surpasses Hester as the fallen woman because his turning away from God is more serious than her transgression against an earthly husband.

In the first chapters of *The Scarlet Letter*, Hester, like her forerunners in Puritan allegory, attempts to desex herself in a repression of individuality which becomes a kind of suicide. Despite her reckless defiance during her trial, Hester accepts society's evaluation of her sexual encounter and seems to relish the role of the fallen woman, not for its identification of her passion but for its condemnation of it. Hester actively participates in her community's attempt to allegorize her "as the figure, the body, the reality of sin."[3] She embroiders the *A* fantastically, dressing Pearl to resemble it in a seemingly rebellious gesture that ultimately indicates her acquiescence. This flagrant behavior not only draws attention to society's interpretation of her, it insists on it. Her refusal to participate in the human community insures her continued allegorical role: "Giving up her individuality, she would become a general symbol at which preachers and moralists might point, and in which they might vivify and embody their images of woman's frailty and sinful passion" (79). That her sexual encounter was adulterous intensifies but does not occasion her discomfort with her own sexuality. Her loveless marriage to Chillingworth suggests Hester's long-standing attempt to repress her passionate and sexual nature. The adulterous act finally forces her to confront her own sexuality but not to approve it.

3. Nathaniel Hawthorne, *The Scarlet Letter*, in *The Works of Nathaniel Hawthorne*, Centenary Edition, ed. Fredson Bowers, 16 vols. (Columbus: Ohio State University Press, 1962), 1:79. All further references to *The Scarlet Letter* will be made to this edition by page number in the text.

Hester cooperates in her punishment by remaining in New England. The narrator, noting that no one requires Hester to stay, offers a series of hypotheses about her motives: a certain "fatality," perhaps, derived from her life's most catastrophic event; her sinful yet intimate connection with Dimmesdale; or what "she compelled herself to believe," what the narrator labels as "half a truth, and half a delusion": "Here, she said to herself, had been the scene of her guilt, and here should be the scene of her earthly punishment" (80). But Hester's reason, qualified by the narrator's romantic vision as "half a truth," speaks convincingly to Hawthorne's presentation of her situation. The two options the narrator suggests are, for Hester, no options at all. He believes that she could return to Europe "and there hide her *character* and identity under a new exterior, as completely as if emerging into another state of being" or could journey into the wilderness, "where *the wildness of her nature* might assimilate itself with a people whose customs and life were alien from the law that had condemned her" (79, italics mine). But when Hester later suggests these options to Dimmesdale, the narrator condemns her, because he recognizes that for Dimmesdale flight would indicate despair. For Hester, newly released from prison, to leave Boston would be a similar gesture of self-condemnation and despair.

If the narrator, removed from the rigors of Puritan social vision by two centuries and a heavy dose of nineteenth-century sentimentality, cannot avoid stereotyping and condemning Hester because she succumbed to sexual passion, how can she, immersed in that cultural perspective, be expected to transcend it immediately and effortlessly? Should she return to Europe, she would indeed live a lie, for Hester believes as much as the narrator that the sexual misstep defines her "character"; she knows, too, that she could not live among "savages": the purported "wildness of her nature" is precisely what she cannot accept, let alone embrace. Chillingworth, not Hester, acknowledges in the prison interview the injustice and unnaturalness of their marriage. Although Hester is a sexual being, she is also a civilized one. She is bound to Boston, to the scene of her "sin," but not for the quasi-mystical reasons the narrator puts for-

ward. Her sense of guilt is acute: "The infant and the shame
were real. Yes!—these were her realities,—all else had van-
ished!" (59). She cannot walk away from her adultery as if it
meant nothing.

The *A* gives Hester a social identity. Like the mark of Cain,
which at once set him apart and protected him, the *A* binds
Hester to the group, even as it limits the kind of social interaction available to her. On the personal level, it gives her an
identity outside of herself, a vantage point from which to objec-
tify herself and to deny that part of her being she cannot accept.
Specifically, it protects her from her own sexuality. The narrator, cataloguing the change in her appearance, concludes:
"There seemed to be no longer anything in Hester's face for love
to dwell upon; nothing in Hester's form, though majestic and
statue-like, that Passion would ever dream of clasping in its
embrace; nothing in Hester's bosom, to make it ever again the
pillow of Affection. Some attribute had departed from her, the
permanence of which had been essential to keep her a woman"
(163). If this were true, Hester's "problem" would be solved: she
would have eradicated her sexual nature. But the process of
allegorization which allows Hester to transcend her "self" prevents her from destroying or denying her sexuality. She becomes "a living sermon against sin," necessarily embodied in
the female; as such, she must continually confront her sexual
nature.

Condemned and self-condemning, Hester, like her lover
Dimmesdale, tries to scourge herself of her sexuality, although
her methods are less overtly violent than his. She moves to an
isolated hut, which the narrator notes for its "comparative
remoteness" and "sterile" soil (81). There she survives on "a
subsistence, of the plainest and most ascetic description,"
wears the "coarsest material" of a "sombre hue." Over the
course of time, Hester adopts the role of a sister of mercy, which
replaces the *A* as a means of effacing her individuality as it more
effectively disguises her sexuality. She forces the community to
think of her asexually, as helper, as nurse; should the role fail to
isolate her adequately, she resorts to the *A* as a shield against
personal contact, for if people "were resolute to accost her, she
laid her finger on the scarlet letter, and passed on" (162).

The narrator acknowledges the motive for Hester's behavior as "an idea of penance" (83) but refuses to credit her with any "genuine and steadfast penitence" (84). He considers her self-denial "morbid," her charity forced, while asserting that "she assumed a freedom of speculation, then common enough on the other side of the Atlantic, but which our forefathers, had they known of it, would have held to be a deadlier crime than that stigmatized by the scarlet letter" (164). Her conformity, he argues, is a sham, for she is impenitent.

Clearly the source of both Hester's compliance and her seeming impenitence is Pearl. The Puritan community attributes the newly acquired "purity of her life" to a real reformation, assuming that "with nothing to lose, in the sight of mankind, and with no hope, and seemingly no wish, of gaining any thing, it could only be a genuine regard for virtue that had brought back the poor wanderer to its path" (160). The narrator, of course, knows better: she could, as the scene at the Governor's Hall shows, lose Pearl. The threat keeps her in line socially, and the narrator believes, Pearl keeps her in line spiritually, not as a Christ figure but as a deterrent: "Had little Pearl never come to her from the spiritual world, it might have been far otherwise. Then, she might have come down to us, hand in hand with Ann Hutchinson, as the foundress of a religious sect" (165). Having to care for Pearl diverts Hester's "enthusiasm of thought" away from the political and theological foundations of the Puritan establishment[4] and onto "the woman problem": "Was existence worth accepting, even to the happiest among them?" (165). In her speculations, Hester imagines that "the whole system of society is to be torn down, and built up anew" (165), but strikingly, in her vision men must only be resocialized; women must change "essentially": they must cease to be women. Commenting on Hester's theory, the narrator suggests that "a woman never overcomes these problems by any exercise of thought. They are not solved, or only in one way. If her heart chance to come uppermost, they vanish" (165). But contrary to the narrator's romantic implication, another kind of love can

---

4. For a complete discussion of the relation between Hester Prynne and Ann Hutchinson, see Colacurcio, "Footsteps of Ann Hutchinson," esp. pp. 466–78.

"save" a woman: Hester loves Pearl. Alone and despairing, Hester considers suicide, but her heart comes uppermost. For Pearl's sake, her meditations do not issue in action.

While the responsibility for a child prevents Hester from becoming politicized, a prophetess in the Ann Hutchinson–Quaker Catharine line, it is, in fact, Pearl who forces Hester's radical critique of Puritan society. Like the love between Edith and Edgar in "The Maypole of Merry Mount," Hester's love for Pearl teaches her how to step out of Puritan typological time into ordinary history.[5] The fact of Pearl ultimately empowers Hester to escape Boston and its definition of reality. She returns not to resume their definition of her but because she understands that she cannot escape her history.[6]

As she allows herself to be allegorized, Hester tries hard to allegorize Pearl. Living in a world that believes spiritual truth expresses itself physically, she distrusts her daughter. The fruit of a sinful act must be sinful or, in fact, sin itself: seductive, foreign yet intimate, and inescapable. At times Pearl seems to Hester as much a monster birth as Hutchinson's "twenty-seven lumps of male seed" seemed to the Puritan community of the 1630s.[7] As such, Hester identifies her with the cloth symbol: "She is the scarlet letter, only capable of being loved, and so endowed with a million-fold the power of retribution for my sin" (113). Hester allows Pearl, as the physical manifestation of her sin, to dominate her and to punish her emotionally.

5. See Colacurcio's discussion of "The Maypole of Merrymount" in *The Province of Piety: Moral History in Hawthorne's Early Tales* (Cambridge: Harvard University Press, 1984), pp. 251–82.

6. Nina Baym comments that Hester's return to New England "admits that the shape of her life has been determined by the interaction between that letter, the social definition of her identity, and her private attempt to withstand that definition" in *The Shape of Hawthorne's Career* (Ithaca: Cornell University Press, 1976), p. 129.

7. John Winthrop quotes John Cotton's suggestion that the miscarriage signified Mrs. Hutchinson's error that "all was Christ in us" (*A Short Story of the Rise, Reign, and Fall of Antinomianism* in *The Antinomian Controversy, 1636–1638: A Documentary History*, ed. David D. Hall [Middletown, Conn.: Wesleyan University Press, 1968]); Cotton Mather considers it evidence of her many heresies, or "false conceptions," turning the tragedy into a huge bio-theological joke. See *Magnalia Christi Americana*, 7 vols. (Hartford, Conn.: Silas Andrus and Sons, 1853), 2:519.

But Pearl is not the Scarlet Letter. She is a child, Hester's pearl "of great price,—purchased with all she had,—her mother's only treasure!" (89). Although Hester often suspects the child, when society threatens to remove Pearl from her care, love prevails. Through Pearl, Hester learns to read the world literally: a child is a child, not an emblem of sin. Because she has Pearl, she can come to recognize that "what we did had a consecration of its own" (195). For Hester, Pearl not only manifests the fact of her "sin" but undermines the community evaluation of that particular sexual act. Because of Pearl, the scarlet letter does not do its "office." Hester remains unrepentant because to repent her "sin" would be to repent Pearl.

Hester's domestication through Pearl not only prevents her from adopting the political role of Ann Hutchinson and the Quaker Catharine; it precludes the role of mortally wounded heroine patterned on Lucrece and Clarissa and manifested in America in Susanna Rowson's *Charlotte Temple*. Clarissa, several weeks after her rape, intimates to Anna Howe that because she now knows that she is not pregnant, she does not have to marry Lovelace: she can act according to her conscience. Conversely, Browning's Pompilia, attempting to will herself to death to escape the brutalities of her husband Guido, experiences a kind of Annunciation, which, with the promise of a new life for which she is responsible, gives her the will not simply to live but to effect her own, and the unborn child's, liberation. Her courage earns her heroic stature. Like Pompilia, Hester has a child to live for, but unlike Pompilia, Hester is not murdered on her childbed. She lives on, effecting a compromise with sexuality, biological process, and generation. In allowing her to do so, Hawthorne writes himself out of a heroine. During the middle of the novel, as Hester lives the uneventful and anonymous life she so desires, she ceases to be heroic.[8] However

8. In "The Gentle Boy" (*Works of Hawthorne*, vol. 9), Dorothy, whom the narrator can only praise by comparing her blameless and uninteresting personality to "a verse of fireside poetry" (85), fades into obscurity despite her faithful stewardship of what the narrator calls "the holiest trust which can be committed to a woman" (95). It is Catharine for whom Ilbrahim waits on his deathbed; it is Catharine who provides the dramatic and moral interest of the

attractive a domesticated woman may seem to the nineteenth-century narrator, her life, like that of the chastened Christiana, does not generate the tension and conflict necessary to literary plotting.

II

Dimmesdale, despite his participation in sex, suffers no physical consequence that would force him to accept his sexual nature. From the beginning of *The Scarlet Letter*, he is torn between his devotion to God and his passion for the world, of which his affair with Hester and his masochism are only "types."[9] Unable to discover a disjunction between his physical and moral nature, Dimmesdale attempts to destroy his body, while searching his soul for evidence of his Election.[10] He is unwilling to believe that actions mean anything, yet he seems incapable of dismissing them. But it is not Dimmesdale's literal adultery that constitutes his idolatry and threatens his spiritual status. The real love triangle in *The Scarlet Letter* does not involve Hester at all. It is Dimmesdale's philosophical speculation with Chillingworth that violates his relationship to God. Dimmesdale's spiritual struggles become the focus of *The Scarlet Letter* as Hawthorne explores Chillingworth's attempt to seduce Dimmesdale, the Bride of Christ, to despair.

Because a man's relationship to God is not defined through his love for and duty toward an earthly spouse, Dimmesdale's sexual encounter with Hester may or may not affect his spiritual state. Chillingworth discovers Dimmesdale obsessed with the spiritual meaning of his physical act; he hopes that

---

story. She obeys a higher law than nineteenth-century domestic sentiment, and she seems to have chosen rightly. What the voice told her when it called her to leave her son—that "his place is here" (87)—proves to be true: even for his infant hands, there was labor in the vineyard.

9. See Frederick Crews, *The Sins of the Fathers* (New York: Oxford University Press, 1966), for a discussion of Dimmesdale's masochism as libidinal repression and displaced sexual gratification.

10. Colacurcio, "Footsteps of Ann Hutchinson," pp. 486–92.

Dimmesdale's preoccupation will blind him to the more serious adultery of their own relationship. Capitalizing on Dimmesdale's commitment to Puritan theology, Chillingworth repeatedly tries to seduce him away from comfort or assurance, from spiritual orthodoxy, to despair. It is an intellectual seduction undertaken for revenge, but in their moments of intense speculation, Chillingworth and Dimmesdale achieve a degree of sinful mutuality that Dimmesdale's sexual union with Hester can only have parodied.[11]

By subterfuge Chillingworth has arranged that he and Dimmesdale take up lodging together. The congregation, disappointed but resigned to Dimmesdale's refusal to marry, "as if priestly celibacy were one of his articles of church-discipline" (125), considers Chillingworth a worthy and acceptable companion; Chillingworth, deprived of the woman "in whom he hoped to find embodied the warmth and cheerfulness of home" (118), finds Dimmesdale a more than adequate substitute. Chillingworth does not claim or avenge himself on Hester because she does not interest him: he never loved her and now finds her foolish and boring. His pride is hurt, not his feelings. The question of Dimmesdale's sanctity provides a new interest "of force enough to engage the full strength of his faculties" (119), both emotional and intellectual.

But Chillingworth's and Dimmesdale's relationship is not only sexually charged; it is intellectually illicit. Their mutual fascination is an attraction of opposites, not simply in character but in profession and, consequently, moral perspective. Dimmesdale, "a true priest, a true religionist, with the reverential sentiment largely developed, and an order of mind that impelled itself powerfully along the track of a creed" (123), feels a fascination "in the man of science, in whom he recognized a cultivation of no moderate depth or scope; together with a range

---

11. Leslie A. Fiedler discusses "the passionate connection" between Dimmesdale and Chillingworth, which seems "an odd combination of the tie between Faust and Gretchen, on the one hand, and Faust and Mephistopheles on the other" in *Love and Death in the American Novel*, rev. ed. (New York: Stein and Day, 1966), p. 234. But Fiedler is too involved in his archetypal reading to recognize the spiritual character of the relationship and love triangle.

and freedom of ideas, that he would have vainly looked for among the members of his own profession" (123). Despite his religious orthodoxy, Dimmesdale finds a "tremulous enjoyment" and "occasional relief" in "looking at the universe through the medium of another kind of intellect than those with which he habitually held converse." (123). In these discussions, Dimmesdale steps outside his creed, outside his faith, if only momentarily. It affects him "as if a window were thrown open, admitting a freer atmosphere into the close and stifled study" (123). It is the air of antinomianism, of Hester's private speculations, a draught of the freer air that Hester and Dimmesdale will breathe during their forest encounter. But it is air "too fresh to be long breathed, with comfort. So the minister, and the physician with him, withdrew within the limits of what their church defined as orthodox" (123–24).

Chillingworth allows Dimmesdale this return to orthodoxy; in fact he even encourages it. He does not wish to free Dimmesdale from the Puritan world view, only to unsettle his understanding of his place within it. He wants Dimmesdale to believe, like Mistress Hibbins and other self-styled witches, that he is damned, that God's saving grace neither can nor will redeem him.[12] In their daily conversations, Chillingworth speaks the language of law, pushing Dimmesdale to confess his conviction of his own damnation within that context. Sensitive to Dimmesdale's fears, he argues against "hypocrisy," a seductive and dangerous argument because, while appearing reasonable, it assumes that deeds provide proof of spiritual status; he insists that penitence before God—private conviction of sin— is inadequate. Dimmesdale at first resists this legalistic vision: "If it be the soul's disease, then I do commit myself to the one Physician of the soul!" His speech reveals his understanding of the sinner's complete dependence on the incomprehensible and unreadable will of God: "Let him do with me as, in his justice

12. Baym points out the distinction between Hester's rebellion and the activity of witches, whose "rebellion arises from accepting the Puritan world view and defining themselves as evil" (*Shape of Hawthorne's Career*, p. 134). She also explores Chillingworth's role as a father figure representing both the superego and Puritan patriarchy.

and wisdom, he shall see good" (137). But Chillingworth keeps pressing him to decide that he can know God's decree, to exalt himself above God by defining his sin as too base to be forgiven.

For Dimmesdale to confess his sin to Chillingworth would mean more than an expression of guilt; it would admit despair, because it would acknowledge the primacy of his physical self. Nina Baym argues that Dimmesdale cannot accept his "passionate core" as the definition of his self. "The part of him that is a Puritan magistrate, and which he thinks of as his 'self,' condemns the sinful 'other.'"[13] Chillingworth posits a psychosomatic origin for Dimmesdale's illness, identifying "a strange sympathy between body and soul" (138), but he believes that he sees mind manifesting its disease physically. Dimmesdale's congregation and clerical superiors are perhaps slightly more aware than Chillingworth of what is really going on: in his self-denial and self-castigation, Dimmesdale's soul is trying to "kill" his body in order to prove to himself that his sexual nature does not define him. He wants to wean his affections from the world. To avenge himself, Chillingworth hopes to keep Dimmesdale alive long enough for his soul to admit defeat. Because an inability to subordinate the flesh to the will of the spirit would constitute defeat, Chillingworth's medical intervention seriously disrupts Dimmesdale's spiritual security.

Chillingworth begins his investigation into Dimmesdale's sanctity, as Lovelace initially approaches Clarissa, "with the severe and equal integrity of a judge, desirous of truth" (129). Lovelace asks whether Clarissa is as pure as she seems to be; Chillingworth asks whether Dimmesdale is the saint or the adulterer. But as Chillingworth proceeds, he loses, like Lovelace, all objectivity: "A terrible fascination, a kind of fierce, though still calm, necessity seized the old man within its gripe, and never set him free again, until he had done all its bidding" (129). The obsession of both seducers with the idea of fixing an immutable identity on their respective victims in turn fixes them.

Chillingworth's uncovering of the sleeping Dimmesdale's

13. Ibid., p. 138.

chest reenacts the rape of Clarissa: both victims are helpless—Clarissa drugged; Dimmesdale in a deep and unnatural slumber, of whose depth Chillingworth seems confident: "Old Roger Chillingworth, without any extraordinary precaution, came into the room. The physician advanced directly in front of his patient, laid his hand on his bosom, and thrust aside the vestment" (138). Chillingworth responds in "a ghastly rapture," an ecstasy that Leslie Fiedler interprets sexually but within the conventional hierarchy that privileges acts of the spirit: "He knows at last the ultimate secret of his dearest enemy; and knowing it, has possessed him, accomplished a rape of the spirit beyond any penetration of the flesh."[14] Certainly Chillingworth believes he has exposed Dimmesdale's true identity as sexual and therefore fallen. That is what Lovelace thought when he raped Clarissa. But Clarissa remains herself, although she can only prove it in dying; Dimmesdale, too, will escape his tormentor's definition. These violations fix the identities of the actors, not of the victims: Lovelace becomes "a rapist," Chillingworth, "a fiend."

Chillingworth's violation of Dimmesdale endows him with a certain coercive power over his victim, not, as in *Clarissa*, because he knows something about his victim but because, for Dimmesdale, Chillingworth's identity is as enigmatic as Lovelace's was to Clarissa before the rape. Before the "rape," Dimmesdale's "sensibility of nerve," or intuition, "would become vaguely aware that something inimical to his peace had thrust itself into relation with him," but "trusting no man as his friend, he could not recognize his enemy when the latter actually appeared" (130). After the event, because he was unconscious when it occurred, Dimmesdale continues to repress his suspicions. Chillingworth's forbidden knowledge, combined with Dimmesdale's ignorance of Chillingworth's true identity, affords him the role of "not a spectator only, but a chief actor, in the poor minister's interior world. He could play upon him as he chose" (140).

14. Fiedler, *Love and Death*, p. 235.

III

In *Love and Death in the American Novel*, Leslie Fiedler describes *The Scarlet Letter* as "a seduction story without a seduction, a parable of the Fall with the Fall offstage and before the action proper." He identifies the action of the romance as "a second temptation, in the face of which his characters, postulated as having been powerless before the 'dark necessity' of their original fall, are portrayed as capable of free choice."[15] In identifying the plot as "a second temptation," however, he suggests that the second recapitulates the first, that Hester's convincing Dimmesdale to run away with her is the outcome most to be feared. This reading casts Hester as the temptress, in the original as in the second "fall," and Chillingworth's instigations toward confession as correct and saving. Yet it seems certain that to credit Chillingworth with either purposefully or inadvertently saving Dimmesdale's soul from Hester's temptation is to misunderstand the text. Such a misreading is understandable. The narrator himself misinterprets the spiritual significance of the forest discussion between Hester and Dimmesdale. But in fact, it is Hester's decision to intervene in the Chillingworth-Dimmesdale relationship that "saves" Dimmesdale from destruction, although not in the way that she had expected.

Hester correctly identifies Chillingworth's influence as the source of Dimmesdale's despondency. She realizes that "besides the legitimate action of his own conscience, a terrible machinery had been brought to bear, and was still operating, on Mr. Dimmesdale's well-being and repose" (158). Predictably, she blames her own "defect of truth" for his psychological and physical decay, as Eve blames herself for Adam's misery after their Fall (*PL* 10.930–31); she decides to inform him of Chillingworth's true identity. The forest interview between Hester and Dimmesdale mirrors the reconciliation scene Milton creates between Adam and Eve. Hester finds Dimmesdale in the forest,

---

15. Ibid., pp. 224, 232.

despairing as Adam does after the Fall. Like Eve, Hester initiates a reconciliation. Like Eve, she is received with abuse and
rejection that couples the woman with the fiend.[16] In *Paradise
Lost*, Adam exclaims, "Out of my sight, thou Serpent, that
name best / Befits thee with him leagu'd, thy self as false / And
hateful" (10.867–69). In *The Scarlet Letter*, when Hester reveals Chillingworth's identity, Dimmesdale responds, "Woman, woman, thou art accountable for this! I cannot forgive
thee!" (194). Like Eve, Hester flings herself at her lover, embraces him, and begs forgiveness, as Eve does in her speech
beginning "Forsake me not thus, Adam" (10.914–36). Like
Adam, Dimmesdale forgives her, and the couple consider their
future, with Hester—again like Eve—suggesting possible solutions. What causes the confusion among critics about how to
read this scene is that Dimmesdale, unlike Adam, listens to
Hester's proposals and seemingly assents. The interview between Hester and Dimmesdale in the forest mirrors the postlapsarian conference between Adam and Eve, except that Dimmesdale takes slightly longer than Adam to decide what course of
action is correct. But by the morning of his Election Day sermon, Dimmesdale, like Adam, "with such counsel nothing
sway'd / To better hopes his more attentive minde / Labouring
had rais'd" (10.1010–12). Like Adam, Dimmesdale successfully
resists a "second temptation," but as in Adam's case, the new
temptation offers not earthly pleasure but despair.

The narrator expresses dismay at the thought of Dimmesdale's flight, but he does so for a reason that misunderstands
both Puritan theology and the complex portrait of Puritan psychology that Hawthorne has drawn in Dimmesdale. The narrator is both literal and romantic. He believes in sacred bonds, in
"the sanctity of the human heart," and in the efficacy of confession: repent and God will forgive you. He assumes that
Dimmesdale's motive and sin in fleeing Boston with Hester
would be sexual. In those terms, he interprets flight as a second
and more serious sin, because it would be a crime not of passion

16. See Roy R. Male, *Hawthorne's Tragic Vision* (Austin: University of
Texas Press, 1957), p. 111.

but of conscious will. But when Dimmesdale responds with horror to the idea of leaving Boston, it is not because he fears giving way to earthly passion. Dimmesdale understands that to decide to leave Boston would be to affirm his own damnation: " 'If, in all these past seven years,' thought he, 'I could recall one instant of peace or hope, I would yet endure, for the sake of that earnest of Heaven's mercy. But now,—since I am irrevocably doomed,—wherefore should I not snatch the solace allowed to the condemned culprit before his execution?' " (201). No matter how tempted he appears to be at this moment, Dimmesdale cannot even express the sinful thought without qualification. He says he has given up on his Election,[17] but he ends his meditation with a prayer: "O Thou to whom I dare not lift mine eyes, wilt Thou yet pardon me!"

Hawthorne describes Dimmesdale's giddiness at this moment in terms of the idolatrous adultery of thought to which Chillingworth has been tempting him in their philosophical discussions. Dimmesdale experiences "the exhilarating effect . . . of breathing the wild, free atmosphere of an unredeemed, unchristianized, lawless region" (201). He defies the spiritual code in which he believes; he also inverts the conventional hierarchy of male-female relationships, the one of which Governor Bellingham reminded him during the initial scaffold scene: "The responsibility of this woman's soul lies greatly with you" (66). Abandoning his responsibility both for himself and for Hester, as Adam abandons his responsibilities when he takes the forbidden fruit from Eve, he speaks of Hester as his savior: "I seem to have flung myself—sick, sin-stained, and sorrow-blackened—down upon these forest leaves, and to have risen up all made anew, and with new powers to glorify Him that hath been merciful" (201–2). But his joy is the giddy recklessness of the damned, and it lasts only briefly. Pearl's return shocks him back into his earlier understanding of the world: "As Arthur Dimmesdale felt the child's eyes upon himself, his hand—with that gesture so habitual as to have become involuntary—stole over his heart" (209). Hester experiences a simi-

17. See Colacurcio, "Footsteps of Hutchinson," p. 491.

lar jolt of reality when Pearl insists that she resume the letter, but to Hester, Pearl is a person. To Dimmesdale, she is a symbol of his sin, capricious, alarming, and threatening to own him.

Hester's decision to speak to Dimmesdale forces him to confront himself and the blasphemy of the despair Chillingworth urged him toward. She provides the occasion for his final trial and his triumph. In resisting the solace embodied in Hester, Dimmesdale affirms his belief in God's ability to save whom he chooses, even adulterous ministers. Hawthorne illustrates Dimmesdale's continuing loyalty to the Puritan system by having him doubt the reality of his experience. Leaving the forest, Dimmesdale looks back, "half expecting that he should discover only some faintly traced features or outline of the mother and child, slowly fading into the twilight of the woods" (214). This impulse suggests a suspicion of specters; he wonders whether he only dreamed of an encounter. In his excited condition, he questions the reality of the town as he approaches; "At every step he was incited to do some strange, wild, wicked thing or other, with a sense that it would be involuntary and irrational" (217). The narrator argues that each impulse arises from deep within Dimmesdale's self, but his language offers another alternative: Dimmesdale may suffer from the Devil's last desperate efforts to win his soul.

The narrator's description of Dimmesdale's response to temptation reveals his inability to distinguish between temptation and sinful assent. In telling terms, the narrator comments on the accident of Dimmesdale's youngest female convert happening to walk by: "Satan, that afternoon, had surely led the poor girl away from her mother's side, and thrown her into the pathway of this *sorely tempted*, or—shall we rather not say?—*this lost and desperate* man" (219, italics mine). But those two phrases mean very different things. The narrator assumes that Dimmesdale has, "as it were," made a pact with the Devil, that, when "the arch-fiend whispered him" some sordid idea, Dimmesdale desired, approved, and relished it. Dimmesdale himself raises this possibility: "What is it that haunts and tempts me thus? . . . Am I mad? or am I given over utterly to the fiend? Did I make a contract with him in the forest, and sign it with my blood?" (220). But according to received tradition, Dimmesdale needn't have "signed a contract" before the Devil could torment him. He neither acts upon nor assents to these wicked thoughts; even if he had, such action would not have "proved" anything to a Calvinist.[18] As Milton has Adam reassure Eve after her dream, "Evil into the mind of God and Man / May come and go, so unapproved, and leave / No spot or blame behind" (5.117–19). Hester urges him to run away; "Satan" encourages blasphemy; but Dimmesdale resists these temptations.

Dimmesdale's Election Sermon confirms his commitment to Puritanism and demonstrates his continuing faith in his own Election. Roy R. Male discusses Dimmesdale's "new vision" as an Emersonian manifesto, as "The Divinity School Address" with a little Manifest Destiny thrown in.[19] But the vision of Dimmesdale's sermon is actually ultraorthodox. He preaches covenant, New England as New Israel, and from what Hester hears from outside the church, the True Sight of Sin—"the complaint of the human heart, sorrow-laden, perchance guilty, telling its secret, whether of guilt or sorrow, to the great heart of mankind" (243). Within the context of orthodox Christianity, there is no reason to doubt Dimmesdale's suspicion that the sermon is divinely inspired. His wonder "that Heaven should see fit to transmit the grand and solemn music of its oracle through so foul an organ-pipe as he" (225) is both conventional self-denigration—he has Saint Paul to imitate—and conventional behavior on Heaven's part.

Because a man displays no visible sign of his particular sexual sin, Dimmesdale is able to adopt the role of the chief of sinners,

18. In his autobiography, *Grace Abounding to the Chief of Sinners*, John Bunyan records fears that "some wicked thought might arise in my heart that might consent thereto; and sometimes also the Tempter would make me believe I had consented to it" (p. 42). Then, at the penultimate moment of the "Sell Christ for this" episode, he relates that "after much striving, even until I was almost out of breath, I felt this thought pass through my heart, *Let him go if he will!* and I thought also that I felt my heart assent freely thereto" (43). He despairs for two years before he begins to experience moments that suggest that the Tempter manufactured this "evil motion" to trick him.

19. Male, *Hawthorne's Tragic Vision*, pp. 114–15.

to claim simultaneously his horrible unworthiness and special election. He emerges from the church triumphant but drained: "The energy—or say, rather, the inspiration which had held him up, until he should have delivered the sacred message that brought its own strength along with it from heaven— was withdrawn" (251). With his remaining strength, Dimmesdale invites Hester and Pearl to accompany him on the scaffold. By taking them with him, Dimmesdale seems to be acknowledging his physical ties, to Hester as his lover and to Pearl as his child. Readers have assumed that he does because they know the "facts." But Dimmesdale's speech and gesture express his relationship to Hester and Pearl metaphorically; he never explicitly acknowledges the literal connection. Instead, Dimmesdale uses Hester as a text, as other preachers have before him. Reducing her to the type of a sinner, he claims to have a far more repulsive and significant letter not on his clothing only or on his mortal flesh but seared on "his inmost heart" (255). His confession has an effect opposite to that of the Reverend Mr. Hooper's sermon from underneath the Black Veil. There, the congregation—enlightened, literal people—tried to attach physical, or "real," meaning to the symbol. Here, the congregation—Puritan, raised on spiritual analogy and hyperbolic expressions of sinful community—interpret the real event symbolically. Dimmesdale "had desired by yielding up his breath in the arms of that fallen woman, to express to the world how utterly nugatory is the choicest of man's own righteousness" (259).

Dimmesdale, I think, anticipates this reaction, because it is spiritually "correct." Had he made his guilty connection to Hester and Pearl explicit and literal, he would have sabotaged his point. Dimmesdale's most spiritual parishioners recognize his death as an educational device: "He had made the manner of his death a parable, in order to impress on his admirers the mighty and mournful lesson, that, in the view of Infinite Purity, we are all sinners alike" (259). He dies believing that he is saved, although he doesn't know about Hester, for her rebellious and impenitent attitude does not indicate to him the presence of prevenient grace, and his vision of eternity is limited. On the scaffold, as in the forest, Dimmesdale tries to correct Hester's understanding of their affair. Then, when Hester cried, "What we did had a consecration of its own" (195), he bade her hush. Now, when she suggests that their mutual suffering has ransomed them, he silences her again. He reminds her of their "sin," offering her as encouragement the record of his own assurances:

> He hath proved His mercy, most of all, in my afflictions. By giving me this burning torture to bear upon my breast! By sending yonder dark and terrible old man, to keep the torture always at red-heat! By bringing me hither to die this death of triumphant ignominy before the people! Had either of these agonies been wanting, I had been lost for ever! Praised be his name! His will be done! Farewell! [256–57]

Dimmesdale has mounted the scaffold triumphantly; he offers Hester the route of triumphant martyrdom. Like Bunyan, he ventures his "eternal state with Christ": "If God doth not come in, thought I, I will leap off the ladder even blindfold into Eternitie, sink or swim, come heaven, come hell; Lord Jesus, if thou wilt catch me, do; if not, I will venture for thy Name."[20] Like Bunyan, Dimmesdale does not know for sure that Christ will catch him, but the Christian does not jump off the ladder knowing that he won't; the Christian jumps on faith, hoping that he will.

Dimmesdale's triumphant death, however, is not available to Hester. She cannot mount the scaffold simultaneously to affirm and deny her passionate nature, because society equates her spiritual and physical states absolutely. She cannot act upon the narrator's suggested moral—"Be true! Be true! Be true! Show freely to the world, if not your worst, yet *some trait whereby the worst may be inferred!*" (260)—because Pearl stands beside her as visible expression of her defining sexuality. In his death, Dimmesdale at once rejects his body and the sexual act that threatened to locate him in it. He kills the "woman" in himself, his sexual, fleshly body, but in the process, like Clarissa and like Georgiana in "The Birthmark" be-

20. Bunyan, *Grace Abounding*, p. 101.

fore him, he kills himself. Hester, burdened with Pearl, has been prevented from pursuing this course. She must remain behind, to carry on as best she can.

IV

At the close of *Middlemarch*, George Eliot remarks, "A new Theresa will hardly have the opportunity of reforming a conventual life, any more than a new Antigone will spend her heroic piety in daring all for the sake of a brother's burial: the medium in which their ardent deeds took shape is forever gone."[21] Like Dorothea, Hester finds the old mediums for heroism unavailable to her, but her failure to achieve heroic or tragic stature as a character derives not only from historical restrictions. Ann Hutchinson and Quaker Catharine have found ways to be heroic; Dimmesdale successfully appropriates the heroine motifs of the eighteenth century. But Hawthorne is reluctant to allow Hester's political consciousness to develop fully.

The depiction of Quaker Catharine in "The Gentle Boy" illustrates Hawthorne's ambivalence about female heroism, particularly when expressed through enthusiasm and prophecy. Catharine, like Hester, has desexed herself. She wears shapeless sackcloth, has strewn ashes in her unkempt hair; her pale face, "emaciated with want, and wild with enthusiasm and strange sorrows, retained no trace of earlier beauty."[22] When she ascends the pulpit, violating traditional sex roles, her unnatural appearance and behavior shocks the minister into "speechless and almost terrified astonishment" (80); she seems a kind of Medusa. The congregation responds to her with the same horror the Puritan divines felt at the trial of Ann Hutchinson; she threatens their political and theological order in the same way.

The narrator in "The Gentle Boy," however, continually undermines our admiration of Catharine. He reports that "when

21. George Eliot, *Middlemarch* (Boston: Houghton Mifflin, 1956), p. 612.
22. Hawthorne, "The Gentle Boy," p. 81, hereafter cited in the text by page number.

her fit of inspiration came. . . . Her discourse gave evidence of an imagination hopelessly entangled with her reason" (81). He dismisses her jeremiad as a "flood of malignity which she mistook for inspiration" (82). Positing the conflict in her life as between "natural duty" and "fanaticism," the narrator affirms that Catharine "violated the duties of the present life and the future by fixing her attention wholly on the latter" (85). Although her understanding of priorities conforms to seventeenth-century practice, the narrator refuses to acknowledge her call. The story vindicates her in leaving Ilbrahim with Dorothy and Tobias but presents her spiritual conviction as dangerously desexing and dehumanizing. The story offers as its religious and heroic ideal Ilbrahim, a gentle boy caught between the poles of Catharine's enthusiasm and Puritan intolerance.

Having saved Hester from the religious heresy of an Ann Hutchinson or the physical tragedy of a Charlotte Temple, Hawthorne seems to feel compelled to rescue her from the social heresy of feminism. He circumscribes Hester's political power by giving her a self-defeating, because literally interpreted, version of Margaret Fuller's prophetic feminism. Margaret Fuller imagines the evolution of human beings and their relationships toward a millennial perfection in which the equality and dignity of Adam and Eve's prelapsarian union would be restored. She urges women to develop their intellects to aid the process of evolution.[23] Hester, too, imagines "that, at some brighter period, when the world should have grown ripe for it, in Heaven's own time, a new truth would be revealed, in order to establish the whole relation between man and woman on a surer ground of mutual happiness" (263). But as the tentativeness of Hester's language indicates, her millennial expectation involves a more restricted course of action.

Hester returns to New England, perhaps motivated, as the narrator suggests, by repentance for her adultery, perhaps simply to resume her place in her personal history. As the narrator

23. Margaret Fuller, "Woman in the Nineteenth Century," in Bell Gale Chevigny, *The Woman and the Myth: Margaret Fuller's Life and Writings* (Old Westbury, N.Y.: Feminist Press, 1976), p. 278.

remarks, "There was more real life for Hester Prynne here, in New England, than in the unknown region where Pearl had found a home" (262–63). Part of Hester's reality is suffering, a suffering linked to the Scarlet Letter, which has become "a type of something to be sorrowed over" (263), a type of "woman's lot." As a young child, Pearl, innocent of the significance of the *A* but curious and perceptive, interpreted it as a symbol of womanhood:

> "I wear nothing on my bosom yet!"
> "Nor ever will my child, I hope," said Hester.
> "And why not, mother?" asked Pearl. . . . "Will it not come of its own accord, when I am a woman grown? [183]

Hester, through her experience of the Scarlet Letter, comes to recognize the universal significance of her mark. She becomes the confidante and counselor of the Salem women, but Hawthorne does not allow her comfort and speculation the energy of her earlier speculations.

Unlike Fuller, who insists, to the point of advocating celibacy, on the need for women to become independent and "self"-centered in order to stand in equal relation to men, Hester advises patience and perseverance within the present patriarchal order until the apocalyptic revelation. The women she counsels are caught "in the continually recurring trials of wounded, wasted, wronged, misplaced, or erring and sinful passion,—or with the dreary burden of a heart unyielded, because unvalued and unsought" (263). They suffer from lovesickness of various sorts and need a man, the "right" man, to set them straight. Such descriptions of the nature of women's dissatisfaction identify marriage as the sole source of earthly fulfillment for women and attempt to reduce all protests against patriarchal suppression of women's minds and wills to a personal emotional complaint. Sophia Hawthorne, writing to her mother about Fuller, articulates this point of view quite decorously: "It seems to me if she were married truly, she would no longer be puzzled about the rights of women. This is the revelation of woman's true destiny and place, which never can be *imagined* by those who do not experience the relation. In perfect, high union there can be no supremacy."[24] Her romantic investment in companionate marriage makes it impossible for her to credit Fuller's social criticism as anything other than spinsterish quibbling.

The ineffectiveness of Hester's feminism derives from the metaphysics of her Puritan heritage, a heritage she shares with the Hawthornes. As a woman, the subordinate and silent half of the couple-body, Hester is excluded from the tradition of prophecy in which Heaven transmits its messages through "foul organ-pipes"; neither can she completely free herself from such a self-denigrating evaluation of her status. Because she is female, Hester cannot find that precedent of grace abounding to the chief of sinners which offers Dimmesdale hope. Unable to transcend her sexual nature, Hester renounces her claim to spiritual insight: "[She] had long since recognized the impossibility that any mission of divine and mysterious truth should be confided to a woman stained with sin, bowed down with shame, or even burdened with a life-long sorrow" (263). Hawthorne gives Hester a vision of Fuller's Virgin Champion without Fuller's understanding that the virginity is spiritual, not physical, that it involves independence, not sexual chastity. Hester imagines her "Virgin Champion" as a chaste married woman, "showing how sacred love should make us happy, by the truest test of a life successful to such an end!" (263). Fuller's vision of the prophetess of sexual equality—virginal, pure, asexual—undercuts her own feminism by idealizing woman as some spiritual, refining force, denying her physical nature and restricting her to a different stereotype. Hester's vision of a prophetess of matrimonial bliss conforms, appropriately, to the seventeenth-century understanding of a woman's purpose and place. But in order to have Hester accept sexual hierarchy as a given, Hawthorne must substitute for her earlier awareness of the need for social reform the fairy-tale solution of romantic love, a solution that is no solution at all.

But despite the retractions and restrictions of the final chapter, Hester's experience and speculations offer a model for a way

24. Sophia Hawthorne to her mother, July 1843, quoted ibid., p. 231.

out of Puritanism. She learns to acknowledge sexuality, generation, and history. As the novel's emphasis on psychology and
the individual undermines the idealizing and stereotyping of
woman inherent in the allegorical world view, the pressure that
the nineteenth-century writer felt to "wrap up the plot" requires a kind of closure that acknowledges history and genera-
tions. Dimmesdale has the big death scene, but Hester remains;
Pearl marries; the female line, at once representative of and
accepting of the body, moves forward in history.

Epilogue

In George Eliot's *Middlemarch*, Dorothea Brooke decides to marry Edward Casaubon because of "childlike ideas about marriage" which she inherits from her Puritan ancestors. She considers marriage a medium for service and self-sacrifice, particularly marriage to a great man "whose odd habits it would have been glorious piety to endure."[1] Intending to be Casaubon's "meet help," she looks forward to "the freedom of voluntary submission to a guide who would take her along the grandest path" (21). Her marriage indeed turns out to be a supreme challenge to her ability to subordinate her own expectations and will, but Casaubon is too emotionally sterile to be a satisfactory spiritual guide. At first, therefore, the story of their marriage seems to be an indictment of the whole idea that women should find their happiness in the service of a man. In the course of the novel, Dorothea moves from one marriage, in which her ideals cause her great pain but allow her a certain tragic grandeur, to another, which meets her expectations of mutuality but reduces her influence and heroic stature.

But the happy ending Eliot denies—a marriage between Dorothea and Lydgate—validates, in the "proper" context, the Pu-

---

1. Eliot, *Middlemarch*, p. 7, hereafter cited by page number in the text.

ritan concept of companionate marriage as an ideal. Married to Lydgate, Dorothea might have put her money and enthusiasm to productive use, to the support and encouragement of a man who deserved her energy. The epic life is denied to Dorothea by a curious combination of forces, a Puritan tradition that has restricted female heroism to self-abnegation in marriage and an author who wishes to expose the damage tradition does to women's spiritual nature. In her Prelude to *Middlemarch*, Eliot writes that young women in her day could not emulate Saint Theresa's heroism because "these latter-born Theresas were helped by no coherent social faith and order which could perform the function of knowledge for the ardently willing soul" (3). But despite Eliot's despair, the Puritan enthusiasm that inspires Dorothea's disastrous first marriage can be recovered for women in a way that allows them heroic activity, because the subordination of women within marriage, an original part of that tradition, is not integral to it.

Because the Pauline texts that shaped Puritan theology continue to shape religious and ethical thought today, Puritan literature evokes uncomfortable responses from modern readers, as it did from Eliot in the nineteenth century. Our tradition asks us to assent to certain of Puritan values, but a newly articulated feminist consciousness demands that we dissent from others. Identifying the feminist critique of Pauline thought as an integral part of the Pauline tradition provides a way to appreciate the complexity and theological richness of these texts without feeling required to condone the doctrines they espouse; it explains and confirms our discomfort. The values to which we assent—the integrity of the individual conscience and the imperative to act according to the dictates of that conscience no matter what the personal risk may be—require and authorize the discomfort we feel with the position of women in these texts. But they offer a model of heroic moral responsibility that can be claimed by women as well as men.

Discussions of women in Puritan texts must avoid apologetics, which Elisabeth Schussler Fiorenza warns does not "take the political implications of scriptural interpretation seriously."[2] They must also eschew contemporary theories about psychology and gender, which sidestep the problem of why these authors thought about women the way they did. Because Puritan literature participates in and attempts to derive its authority from the ideology of biblical patriarchy and because that ideology continues to shape our culture, these texts remain immensely powerful. Both apologetics and feminist criticism that approach Puritan literature from outside the Pauline tradition risk leaving the central contradictions of the texts intact. They force the reader either to accept the text on all of its own terms or to reject it without examining how the assumptions in the text continue to operate today. Only by approaching them from within the Pauline context can criticism effectively expose the true shape of both their oppression and their fascination. An informed Puritan critique allows us to reclaim the literature of individual conscience and impassioned protest by using its own tools to expose and neutralize its disfiguring ideological assumptions.

2. Fiorenza, *Bread Not Stone,* p. 53.

Bibliography

Adams, Richard. "How may child-bearing women be most encouraged and supported against, in, and under the hazard of their travail?" In *Puritan Sermons, 1659–1689*. Wheaton, Ill.: Robert Owen Roberts, 1981.

Aers, David, and Robert Hodge. "'Rational Burning': Milton on Sex and Marriage." *Milton Studies* 13. Ed. James D. Simmonds. Pittsburgh: University of Pittsburgh Press, 1979.

Ames, William. *The Marrow of Theology*. Trans. from the 3d Latin edition (1629) and ed. John D. Eusden. Durham, N.C.: Labyrinth Press, 1968.

Ashbridge, Elizabeth. *Some Account of the Life of Elizabeth Ashbridge, written by herself*. Philadelphia: Friends' Book Store, [1808?].

Bayly, Lewis. *The Practise of Piety, Directing a Christian how to walk with God*. London, 1612. Available through the Short Title Catalogue Microfilm series.

Baym, Nina. *The Shape of Hawthorne's Career*. Ithaca: Cornell University Press, 1976.

Becker, John E. *Hawthorne's Historical Allegory: An Examination of the American Conscience*. Port Washington, N.Y.: Kennikat Press, 1971.

Beer, Gillian. "Richardson, Milton, and the Status of Evil." *Review of English Studies* 19 (1968).

Bell, Michael Davitt. *Hawthorne and the Historical Romance of New England*. Princeton: Princeton University Press, 1971.

Belson, Joel Jay. "The Names in *The Faerie Queene*." Ph.D. diss., Columbia University, 1964.

Booty, John E., ed. *The Book of Common Prayer, 1559: The Elizabethan Prayer Book*. Charlottesville: University Press of Virginia, 1976.

Bradstreet, Anne. *The Works of Anne Bradstreet*. Ed. Jeannine Hensley. Cambridge: Belknap Press of Harvard University, 1967.

Buell, Lawrence. "Rival Romantic Interpretations of New England Puritanism: Hawthorne versus Stowe." *Texas Studies in Literature and Language* 25 (1983).

Bunyan, John. *Grace Abounding to the Chief of Sinners*. Ed. Roger Sharrock. Oxford: Clarendon Press, 1962.

——. *The Life and Death of Mr. Badman*. London: Oxford University Press, 1929.

——. *The Pilgrim's Progress*. Ed. Roger Sharrock. New York: Penguin Books, 1965.

——. *The Poems*. Ed. Graham Midgley. Oxford: Clarendon Press, 1980.

——. *The Works of John Bunyan*. 3 vols. Ed. George Offor. Glasgow: Blackie and Son, 1856.

Burden, Dennis. *The Logical Epic: A Study of the Argument of Paradise Lost*. Cambridge: Harvard University Press, 1967.

Butler, Janet. "The Garden: Early Symbol of Clarissa's Complicity." *Studies in English Literature* 24 (1984).

Calvin, John. *Institutes of the Christian Religion*. 2 vols. Trans. Henry Beveridge. Grand Rapids, Mich.: Wm. B. Eerdman, 1953.

Castle, Terry. *Clarissa's Ciphers: Meaning and Disruption in Richardson's "Clarissa."* Ithaca: Cornell University Press, 1982.

Cheney, Donald. "Spenser's Hermaphrodite and the 1590 *Faerie Queene*." *PMLA* 87 (1972).

Chevigny, Bell Gale. *The Woman and the Myth: Margaret Fuller's Life and Writings*. Old Westbury, N.Y.: Feminist Press, 1976.

Clifford, Gay. *The Transformations of Allegory*. London: Routledge and Kegan Paul, 1974.

Colacurcio, Michael J. "Footsteps of Ann Hutchinson." *English Literary History* 39 (1972).

——. *The Province of Piety: Moral History in Hawthorne's Early Tales*. Cambridge: Harvard University Press, 1984.

Coolidge, John S. *The Pauline Renaissance in England: Puritanism and the Bible*. Oxford: Clarendon Press, 1970.

Crews, Frederick. *The Sins of the Fathers*. New York: Oxford University Press, 1966.

Crosman, Robert. *Reading Paradise Lost*. Bloomington: Indiana University Press, 1980.

Davies, Horton. *Worship and Theology in England: From Andrews to Baxter*. 5 vols. Princeton: Princeton University Press, 1975.

Donaldson, Ian. "Fielding, Richardson, and the Ends of the Novel." *Essays in Criticism* 32 (1982).

Doody, Margaret Anne. *A Natural Passion: A Study of the Novels of Samuel Richardson.* Oxford: Clarendon Press, 1974.

DuPlessis, Rachel Blau. *Writing beyond the Ending: Narrative Strategies of Twentieth-Century Women Writers.* Bloomington: Indiana University Press, 1985.

Dussinger, John A. "Love and Consanguinity in Richardson's Novels." *Studies in English Literature* 24 (1984).

Eagleton, Terry. *The Rape of Clarissa: Writing, Sexuality, and Class Struggle.* Minneapolis: University of Minnesota, 1982.

Elredge, Patricia Reid. "Karen Horney and *Clarissa*: The Tragedy of Neurotic Pride." *American Journal of Psychoanalysis* 42 (1982).

Fetterley, Judith. *The Resisting Reader: A Feminist Approach to American Literature.* Bloomington: Indiana University Press, 1978.

Fiedler, Leslie A. *Love and Death in the American Novel.* Rev. ed. New York: Stein and Day, 1966.

Fiorenza, Elisabeth Schussler. *Bread Not Stone: The Challenge of Feminist Biblical Interpretation.* Boston: Beacon Press, 1984.

The First Prayer-Book as issued by the Authority of the Parliament of the Second Year of King Edward VI. London: Simkin, Marshall, 1912.

Fish, Stanley. *Self-Consuming Artifacts.* Berkeley: University of California Press, 1972.

——. *Surprised by Sin: The Reader in Paradise Lost.* London: Macmillan, 1967.

Fletcher, Angus. *Allegory: The Theory of a Symbolic Mode.* Ithaca: Cornell University Press, 1964.

Foxe, John. *Acts and Monuments* (1563). In *Foxe's Book of Martyrs.* Ed. and abr. G. A. Williamson. London: Secker and Warburg, 1965.

Frere, W. H., and C. E. Douglas, eds. *Puritan Manifestoes: A Study of the Origin of the Puritan Revolt, with a reprint of the Admonition to Parliament and kindred documents, 1572.* London: Society for Promoting Christian Knowledge, 1907.

Fresch, Cheryl Hope. "Milton's Eve and the Theological Tradition." Ph.D. diss., Cornell University, 1976.

Freud, Sigmund. *Moses and Monotheism.* Trans. Katherine Jones. New York: Vintage Press, 1967.

Froula, Christine. "When Eve Reads Milton: Undoing the Canonical Economy." *Critical Inquiry* 10 (1983).

Frye, Roland. *God, Man, and Satan.* Princeton: Princeton University Press, 1960.

Furlong, Monica. *Puritan's Progress: A Study of John Bunyan.* London: Hodder and Stoughton, 1975.

Gilbert, Sandra. "Patriarchal Poetry and Women Readers: Reflections on Milton's Bogey." *PMLA* 93 (1978).

Gouge, William. *Of Domesticall Duties* (London, 1622). Reproduced from the Bodleian Library copy. Amsterdam: Theatrum Orbis Terrarum, 1976.

Hagstrum, Jean H. *Sex and Sensibility: Ideal and Erotic Love from Milton to Mozart.* Chicago: University of Chicago Press, 1980.

Halkett, John. *Milton and the Idea of Matrimony: A Study of the Divorce Tracts and "Paradise Lost."* New Haven: Yale University Press, 1970.

Hall, David D., ed. *The Antinomian Controversy, 1636–1638: A Documentary History.* Middletown, Conn.: Wesleyan University Press, 1968.

Haller, William, and Malleville Haller. "The Puritan Art of Love." *Huntington Library Quarterly* 5 (1942).

Hamilton, A. C. *The Structure of Allegory in "The Faerie Queene."* Oxford: Clarendon Press, 1961.

Hankins, John E. "Spenser and the Revelation of St. John." In *Essential Articles for the Study of Edmund Spenser.* Ed. A. C. Hamilton. Hamden, Conn.: Archon, 1972.

Hawthorne, Nathaniel. *The Works of Nathaniel Hawthorne.* Centenary Edition. 16 vols. Ed. Fredson Bowers. Columbus: Ohio State University Press, 1962.

Hieatt, A. Kent. *Chaucer, Spenser, Milton: Mythopoeic Continuites and Transformations.* Montreal: McGill-Queen's University Press, 1975.

Hill, Christopher. *Puritanism and Revolution: Studies in Interpretation of the English Revolution of the Seventeenth Century.* London: Secker and Warburg, 1958.

——. *The World Turned Upside Down: Radical Ideas during the English Revolution.* London: Temple Smith, 1972.

Hume, Anthea. *Edmund Spenser: Protestant Poet.* Cambridge: Cambridge University Press, 1984.

Jardine, Lisa. *Still Harping on Daughters: Women and Drama in the Age of Shakespeare.* Totowa, N.J.: Barnes and Noble, 1983.

Kaufmann, U. Milo. *"The Pilgrim's Progress" and Traditions in Puritan Meditation.* New Haven: Yale University Press, 1966.

Keeble, N. H. "Christiana's Key: The Unity of *The Pilgrim's Progress.*" In *"The Pilgrim's Progress": Critical and Historical Views.* Ed. Vincent Newey. Totowa, N.J.: Barnes and Noble, 1980.

Knott, John R. Jr. "Bunyan and the Holy Community." *Studies in Philology* 80 (Spring 1983).

——. *The Sword of the Spirit: Puritan Responses to the Bible.* Chicago, Ill.: University of Chicago Press, 1980.

Kranidas, Thomas, ed. *New Essays on Paradise Lost.* Berkeley: University of California Press, 1969.

Lewis, C. S. *The Allegory of Love: A Study in Medieval Tradition.* London: Oxford University Press, 1936.

Loesberg, Jonathan. "Allegory and Narrative in *Clarissa.*" *Novel* 15 (1981).

Luther, Martin. *Luther's Works*. Ed. Jaroslav Pelikan. St. Louis: Concordia, 1963.

MacCaffrey, Isabel. *Spenser's Allegory: The Anatomy of Imagination*. Princeton: Princeton University Press, 1976.

McColley, Diane Kelsey. "Eve's Dream." *Milton Studies* 12. Ed. James D. Simmonds. Pittsburgh: University of Pittsburgh Press, 1978.

——. "Free Will and Obedience in the Separation Scene of *Paradise Lost.*" *Studies in English Literature* 12 (1972).

——. *Milton's Eve*. Urbana: University of Illinois Press, 1983.

McGuire, Maryann. *Milton's Puritan Masque*. Athens: University of Georgia Press, 1983.

Maddox, James. "Lovelace and the World of Ressentiment in *Clarissa.*" *Texas Studies in Literature and Language* 24 (1982).

Mahl, Mary R., and Helene Koon, eds. *The Female Spectator*. Old Westbury, N.Y.: The Feminist Press, 1977.

Male, Roy R. *Hawthorne's Tragic Vision*. Austin: University of Texas Press, 1957.

Mather, Cotton. *Bethiah: The Glory which Adorns the Daughters of God* (Boston 1722). Evans American Bibliography, Catalogue #2353.

——. "Elizabeth in her Holy Retirement" (Boston, 1710). Evans American Bibliography, Catalogue #1463.

——. *Magnalia Christi Americana*. 7 vols. Hartford, Conn.: Silas Andrus and Sons, 1853.

——. "Ornaments for the Daughters of Zion" (Boston, 1692). Evans American Bibliography, Catalogue #624.

Miller, Nancy K. *The Heroine's Text: Readings in the French and English Novel, 1722–1782*. New York: Columbia University Press, 1980.

Miller, Perry, ed. *The American Puritans: Their Poetry and Prose*. Garden City, N.Y.: Doubleday, 1956.

——. *Errand into the Wilderness*. Cambridge: Belknap Press of Harvard University Press, 1956.

Milton, John. *Complete Shorter Poems*. Ed. John Carey. London: Longman Group, 1971.

——. *The Complete Works of John Milton*. Ed. Frank Allen Paterson. New York: Columbia University Press, 1931.

——. *Paradise Lost*. Ed. Alastair Fowler. London: Longman, 1971.

Morgan, Edmund. *The Puritan Dilemma: The Story of John Winthrop*. Boston: Little, Brown, 1958.

——. *The Puritan Family*. Boston: Trustees of the Public Library, 1944.

——. *Visible Saints: The History of a Puritan Idea*. Ithaca: Cornell University Press, 1965.

Murrin, Michael. *The Allegorical Epic: Essays in Its Rise and Decline.* Chicago: University of Chicago Press, 1980.

Nohrnberg, James. *The Analogy of "The Faerie Queene."* Princeton: Princeton University Press, 1976.

Oliver, John. *A Present to be given to Teeming Women* (London 1669). Courtesy of the Burke Library of Union Theological Seminary.

Oram, William A. "Characterization and Spenser's Allegory." In *Spenser at Kalamazoo, 1984.* Clarion: Clarion University of Pennsylvania, 1984.

Overbury, Thomas. *The Miscellaneous Works in Prose and Verse of Sir Thomas Overbury, Knt.* Ed. Edward F. Rimbault. London: Reeves and Turner, 1890.

Patrides, C. A., ed. *Approaches to Paradise Lost.* London: Edward Arnold, 1968.

Paul. *The Writings of St. Paul.* Ed. Wayne Meeks. New York: W. W. Norton, 1972.

Perkins, Williams. *The Works of that famous and worthy minister of Christ in the Universitie of Cambridge, M. W. Perkins. The Third and Last Volume.* Cambridge: Cantrell Legge, Printer to the Universitie of Cambridge, 1618.

Poovey, Mary. "Journeys from This World to the Next: The Providential Promise in *Clarissa* and *Tom Jones.*" *ELH* 43 (1976).

Proctor, Francis, and Walter Frere. *A New History of the Book of Common Prayer.* London: Macmillan, 1961.

Quilligan, Maureen. *The Language of Allegory: Defining the Genre.* Ithaca: Cornell University Press, 1979.

——. *Milton's Spenser: The Politics of Reading.* Ithaca: Cornell University Press, 1983.

Radzinowicz, Mary Ann. *Toward "Samson Agonistes": The Growth of Milton's Mind.* Princeton: Princeton University Press, 1978.

Revard, Stella P. "Eve and the Doctrine of Responsibility in *Paradise Lost.*" *PMLA* 88 (1973).

Richardson, Samuel. *Clarissa.* 4 vols. London: J. M. Dent and Sons, 1932.

Roche, Thomas P., Jr. *The Kindly Flame: A Study of the Third and Fourth Books of Spenser's "Faerie Queene."* Princeton: Princeton University Press, 1964.

Rose, Mark. *Heroic Love: Studies in Sidney and Spenser.* Cambridge: Harvard University Press, 1968.

Ruether, Rosemary Radford, and Eleanor McLaughlin, eds. *Women of Spirit: Female Leadership in the Jewish and Christian Traditions,* New York: Simon and Schuster, 1977.

Russell, Letty M. *Feminist Interpretation of the Bible.* Philadelphia: Westminster Press, 1985.

Sadler, Lynn Veach. *John Bunyan.* Boston: Twayne, 1979.

Safer, Elaine. "'Sufficient to Have Stood': Eve's Responsibility in Book IX." *Milton Quarterly* 6 (1972).

Scholes, Robert, and Robert Kellogg. *The Nature of Narrative*. New York: Oxford University Press, 1966.

Scholten, Catherine. *Childbearing in American Society, 1650–1850*. New York: New York University Press, 1985.

Sharrock, Roger, ed. *Bunyan, "The Pilgrim's Progress": A Casebook*. London: Macmillan, 1976.

Spenser, Edmund. *Spenser: Poetical Works*. Ed. J. C. Smith and E. de Selincourt. London: Oxford University Press, 1912.

——. *The Works of Edmund Spenser: A Variorum Edition*. Ed. Frederick M. Padelford. Baltimore: Johns Hopkins University Press, 1934.

Stedman, Edmund Clarence, and Ellen Mackay Hutchinson, Eds. *A Library of American Literature from the Earliest Settlement to the Present Time*. 11 vols. New York: Charles L. Webster, 1891.

Stevenson, John Allen. "The Courtship of the Family: Clarissa and the Harlowes Once More." *ELH* 48 (1981).

Stone, Lawrence. *Family, Sex, and Marriage, 1500–1800*. New York: Harper and Row, 1977.

Summers, Joseph. *The Muse's Method: An Introduction to "Paradise Lost."* Cambridge: Harvard University Press, 1962.

Taylor, Jeremy. *The Whole Works of the Right Reverend Jeremy Taylor, D.D.* 15 vols. Ed. Reginald Heber. London: Ogle, Duncan, 1822.

Van Dyke, Carolynn. *The Fiction of Truth: Structures of Meaning in Narrative and Dramatic Allegory*. Ithaca: Cornell University Press, 1985.

Van Ghent, Dorothy. *The English Novel: Form and Function*. New York: Harper Torchbooks, 1953.

Wadsworth, Benjamin. *The Well-Ordered Family* (Boston, 1712). Evans American Bibliography, Catalogue #1591.

Waggoner, Hyatt H. *Hawthorne: A Critical Study*. Rev. ed. Cambridge: Belknap Press of Harvard University Press, 1963.

Warner, William Beatty. *Reading "Clarissa": The Struggle of Interpretation*. New Haven: Yale University Press, 1979.

——. "Reading Rape: Marxist-Feminist Configurations of the Literal." *Diacritics* (Winter 1983).

Watt, Ian. *The Rise of the Novel: Studies in Defoe, Richardson, and Fielding*. Berkeley: University of California Press, 1957.

Webber, Joan. "The Politics of Poetry: Feminism and *Paradise Lost*." *Milton Studies* 14. Ed. James D. Simmonds. Pittsburgh: University of Pittsburgh Press, 1980.

White, Peter. "The Monstrous Birth and 'The Gentle Boy': Hawthorne's Use of the Past." *Nathaniel Hawthorne Journal* (1976).

Williams, Kathleen. *Spenser's World of Glass: A Reading of "The Faerie Queene."* Berkeley: University of California Press, 1966.

Willis, Gladys J. *The Penalty of Eve: John Milton and Divorce.* New York: Peter Lang, 1984.

Wilt, Judith. "He Could Go No Farther: A Modest Proposal about Lovelace and Clarissa." *PMLA* 92 (1977).

Winthrop, John. *The History of New England from 1630–1649, from his original manuscripts.* 2 vols. Ed. James Savage. Boston: Phelps and Farnham, 1825.

Wolff, Cynthia Griffin. *Samuel Richardson and the Eighteenth-Century Puritan Character.* Hamden, Conn.: Archon, 1972.

Index

Library of Congress Cataloging-in-Publication Data

Thickstun, Margaret Olofson, 1956–
    Fictions of the feminine: Puritan doctrine and the representation
of women/Margaret Olofson Thickstun.
        p.   cm.
    Bibliography: p.
    Includes index.
    ISBN 0-8014-2107-1 (alk. paper)
    1. English literature—History and criticism.   2. Women in
literature.   3. Woman (Christian theology) in literature.
4. English literature—Puritan authors—History and criticism.
5. Puritans in literature.   6. Hawthorne, Nathaniel, 1804–1864.
Scarlet letter.   7. Feminism and literature.   8. Sex role in
literature.   I. Title.
PR151.W6T48   1988
820'.9'352042—dc19   87-25072